MathFlare

Name: ______________________________

Class: ____________

Teacher: ______________________________

Introduction

As parents and educators, we recognize the pivotal role mathematics plays in shaping a child's academic journey and future success. Yet, the path to mathematical proficiency can often seem daunting, fraught with challenges and complexities. That's where the transformative power of MathFlare Workbooks shine through, illuminating the way forward with clarity, precision, and purpose.

Introducing MathFlare Workbooks – a beacon of guidance, a testament to excellence, and a catalyst for achievement. Crafted with meticulous care and expertise, MathFlare Workbooks stand as paragons of educational excellence, designed to nurture young minds, ignite a passion for learning, and develop a deep-rooted understanding of mathematical concepts.

Picture this: your child eagerly delves into the pages of Mathflare Workbook, greeted by a step-by-step guide illuminated with vivid examples that demystify complex mathematical concepts. With each turn of the page, they embark on a journey of discovery, encountering thoughtfully curated practice questions that reinforce learning and hone problem-solving skills. And when they unveil the answers to those very questions, a sense of accomplishment blossoms within them – a tangible reward for their hard work and dedication.

But MathFlare Workbooks are more than just tools for learning; they are pathways to comprehension, fostering a deep-seated understanding of mathematical concepts through a sequential, logical flow. From fundamental principles to advanced problem-solving strategies, every chapter builds upon the last, ensuring a robust foundation upon which future knowledge can be constructed.

As parents, we yearn for nothing more than to see our children thrive, to witness the spark of inspiration ignited within them as they conquer academic challenges with confidence and poise. MathFlare Workbooks serve as partners in this noble endeavor, offering not just practice questions, but the keys to unlocking a world of opportunity.

And for teachers, MathFlare Workbooks stand as invaluable allies in the quest to cultivate mathematical proficiency in the classroom. With answers readily available, instructors can focus on guiding and nurturing their students, confident in the knowledge that MathFlare Workbooks provide a solid framework upon which to build.

In the pages of MathFlare Workbooks, we find not just the promise of academic excellence, but the seeds of a brighter tomorrow. So let us embrace the power of mathematics, let us champion the journey of learning, and let us pave the way for a generation of young minds poised to shape the world. With MathFlare Workbooks as our guide, the possibilities are infinite, and the future, bright.

Table of Contents

MathFlare
MATH WORKBOOK
Grade 2
Addition Subtraction
Multiplication
Place Value and Expanded Notations
Geometry
Step by Step Guide and Essential Practice with Answers
MathFlare Publishing

MathFlare
MATH WORKBOOK
Grade 2-3
Addition Subtraction
Multiplication and Division
Place Value and Expanded Notations
Geometry
Step by Step Guide and Essential Practice with Answers
MathFlare Publishing

MathFlare
MATH WORKBOOK
Grade 3
Multiplication and Division
Decimals
Place Value and Expanded Notations
Fractions and Geometry
Step by Step Guide and Essential Practice with Answers
MathFlare Publishing

MathFlare
MATH WORKBOOK
Grade 1
Counting and Numbers
Addition and Subtraction
Place Value and Expanded Notations
Understanding Time
Step by Step Guide and Essential Practice with Answers
MathFlare Publishing

MathFlare
MATH WORKBOOK
Grade 1-2
Counting and Numbers
Addition and Subtraction
Place Value and Expanded Notations
Understanding Time
Step by Step Guide and Essential Practice with Answers
MathFlare Publishing

MathFlare
MATH WORKBOOK
Grade 3-4
Addition Subtraction
Multiplication Division
Place Value and Expanded Notations
Fractions and Geometry
Step by Step Guide and Essential Practice with Answers
MathFlare Publishing

MathFlare
MATH WORKBOOK
Grade 4
Addition Subtraction
Multiplication Division
Place Value and Expanded Notations
Fractions and Geometry
Step by Step Guide and Essential Practice with Answers
MathFlare Publishing

MathFlare
MATH WORKBOOK
Grade 4-5
Multiplication Division
Place Value and Expanded Notations
Fractions and Geometry
Unit Conversion
Step by Step Guide and Essential Practice with Answers
MathFlare Publishing

MathFlare
MATH WORKBOOK
Grade 5
Step by Step Guide and Essential Practice with Answers
Multiplication Division
Place Value and Expanded Notations
Fractions and Geometry
Unit Conversion
MathFlare Publishing

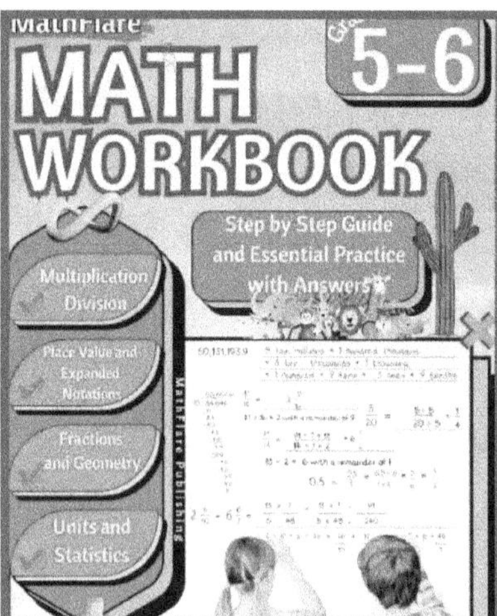
MathFlare
MATH WORKBOOK
Grade 5-6
Step by Step Guide and Essential Practice with Answers
Multiplication Division
Place Value and Expanded Notations
Fractions and Geometry
Units and Statistics
MathFlare Publishing

MathFlare
MATH WORKBOOK
Grade 6
Step by Step Guide and Essential Practice with Answers
Integers and Statistics
Arithmetic and Pre-Algebra
Fractions and Geometry
Ratio and Percentage
MathFlare Publishing

MathFlare
MATH WORKBOOK
Grade 6-7
Step by Step Guide and Essential Practice with Answers
Arithmetic and Pre-Algebra
Ratio, Percent Proportion
Geometry
Statistics
MathFlare Publishing

MathFlare
MATH WORKBOOK
Grade 7
Step by Step Guide and Essential Practice with Answers
Pre-Algebra
Ratio, Percent Proportion
Geometry
Statistics
MathFlare Publishing

MathFlare
MATH WORKBOOK
Grade 7-8
Step by Step Guide and Essential Practice with Answers
Pre-Algebra
Ratio, Percent Proportion
Geometry and Cartesian Plane
Statistics
MathFlare Publishing

MathFlare
MATH WORKBOOK
Grade 8-9
Step by Step Guide and Essential Practice with Answers
Pre-Algebra
Ratio, Proportion and Percentage
Linear Equations
Geometry and Cartesian Plane
MathFlare Publishing

MathFlare
MATH WORKBOOK
Grade 8
Step by Step Guide and Essential Practice with Answers
Pre-Algebra
Percentage
Linear Equations
Geometry
MathFlare Publishing

Evaluate Expressions

Evaluating expressions involves substituting given values for variables in an expression and then performing the indicated operations to find the result.

For example: Let's evaluate 4x – 10, when x = 3:

Step 1: Substitute the given value for the variable:

Replace every occurrence of x in the expression 4x – 10 with the given value, which is 3:

$$= 4(3) - 10$$

Step 2: Perform the operations:

Perform the indicated operations according to the order of operations (PEMDAS - Parentheses, Exponents, Multiplication and Division, Addition and Subtraction):

$$= 4 \times 3 - 10$$

Step 3: Simplify:

Calculate the result:

$$12 - 10 = 2$$

Solving Equations (One Side)

Solving one-step equations involves performing a single operation to isolate the variable and find its value.

Let's solve an equation step by step: 16 + x = 31

1. **Identify the Goal:**

    The goal is to isolate the variable x on one side of the equation.

2. **Simplify the Equation**: Combine like terms on both sides of the equation, if necessary.

> The equation is already simplified.

3. **Undo Addition or Subtraction**: If there's addition or subtraction involving the variable, undo it by performing the opposite operation on both sides of the equation.

> Since x is being added to 16, we'll undo this operation by subtracting 16 from both sides of the equation:

$$16 + x - 16 = 31 - 16$$

4. **Isolate the Variable**: Ensure that the variable is alone on one side of the equation.

$$X = 15$$

5. **Check Your Solution**: Substitute the value of x back into the original equation to verify that it satisfies the equation.

$$16 + 15 = 31$$

$$31 = 31$$

The equation is balanced, so the solution.

Equations (Two Sides)

A two-sided equation is an equation where both sides have expressions with variables and constants. The goal when solving a two-sided equation is to find the value of the variable that makes both sides equal.

For example: Let's solve an equation:

$$9 + 8x + 8 = 64 + x + 2$$

- **Combine Like Terms:** Simplify each side of the equation by combining like terms (terms with the same variable or constants).

$$9 + 8x + 8 = 64 + x + 2$$

$$17 + 8x = 66 + x$$

- **Isolate the Variable:** Use inverse operations to isolate the variable on one side of the equation.

subtract x from both sides:

$$17 + 8x - x = 66 + x - x$$

$$17 + 7x = 66$$

subtracting 17 from both sides:

$$17 - 17 + 7x = 66 - 17$$

$$7x = 49$$

divide both sides by 7:

$$\frac{7x}{7} = \frac{49}{7} = x = 7$$

- **Check Solution:** Once you find the solution, substitute it back into the original equation to ensure it makes the equation true.

Substitute $x = 7$ back into the original equation:

$$9 + 8(7) + 8 = 64 + 7 + 2$$

$$9 + 56 + 8 = 64 + 7 + 2$$

$$73 = 73$$

<u>Find Numbers (Verbal Algebra)</u>

Verbal algebra involves translating word problems or verbal statements into algebraic expressions or equations.

For example: The product of the two numbers is 91. One number is six less than the other. What are the numbers?

We're given a verbal description of a problem, and we need to represent it using algebraic symbols and equations.

Let's break down the given problem into algebraic expressions:

- Given that the product of the two numbers is 91, we can write the equation: $xy = 91$
- Also, given that one number is six less than the other, we can write another equation: $x = y - 6$

Now, we can use algebraic techniques to solve the system of equations to find the values of x and y, which represent the two numbers.

$$x(x - 6) = 91$$

1. Solve the equation:

    - Expand the equation:

    $$x^2 - 6x = 91$$

    - Rearrange the equation into standard quadratic form:

    $$x^2 - 6x - 91 = 0$$

    - Factor the quadratic equation:

    $$(x - 13)(x + 7) = 0$$

2. Find the solutions for x:

- From the factored form, we have two possible values for x:

$$x = 13 \text{ or } x = -7$$

3. **Check the validity of the solutions:**

   - Since one number is six less than the other, we discard the negative solution.

   - Therefore, the solution is $x = 13$.

4. **Find the other number:**

   - Substitute $x = 13$ into the expression for the other number:

   Other number $= x - 6 = 13 - 6 = 7$

So, the two numbers are 13 and 7.

Solving Inequalities

Inequalities are mathematical expressions that compare the relative sizes of two values. They are used to express relationships where one quantity is:

- "$<$" (less than),
- "$>$" (greater than),
- "$<=$" (less than or equal to),
- "$>=$" (greater than or equal to),
- and "$\neq$" (not equal to) another quantity.

For example:

$$y + {-10} \leq {-8}$$

To isolate y, we need to get rid of the constant term -10. Since -10 is being subtracted from y, we can undo this operation by adding 10 to both sides of the inequality:

$$y - 10 + 10 \le -8 + 10$$

$$y \le 2$$

To check the solution:

$$2 - 10 \le -8$$

$$-8 = -8$$

The inequality is true when $y = 2$

Linear Equation

A linear equation is an algebraic equation that represents a straight line when graphed on a coordinate plane. It consists of variables raised to the power of 1 (i.e., no exponents higher than 1) and constant coefficients.

The general form of a linear equation in one variable x is:

$$ax + b = 0$$

Where a and b are constants, and x is the variable.

Let's solve the linear equation:

$$-2x + 9 = 5$$

- **Isolate the variable term:** We want to isolate the term containing x on one side of the equation. To do this, we'll move the constant term to the other side. Subtract 9 from both sides:

$$-2x + 9 - 9 = 5 - 9$$

$$-2x = -4$$

- **Divide by the coefficient of the variable:** To solve for x, divide both sides by the coefficient of x, which is -2:
$$\frac{-2x}{-2} = \frac{-4}{-2}$$

$$x = 2$$

<u>Slop from Two Points</u>

The slope between two points on a Cartesian coordinate system is a measure of the steepness of the line connecting those points. It's calculated by finding the change in the y-coordinates divided by the change in the x-coordinates.

- The coordinates of the first point as $(x_1, y_1) = (2, -30)$.

- The coordinates of the second point as $(x_2, y_2) = (-5, 40)$.

The formula to calculate the slope (m) between two points:

$$\frac{y2 - y1}{x2 - x1}$$

$$= \frac{40 - (-30)}{-5 - 2} = \frac{70}{-7}$$

$$\text{Slope} = -10$$

Quadratic Equations

A quadratic equation is a polynomial equation of the second degree, meaning it can be written in the form:

$$ax^2 + bx + c = 0$$

where a, b, and c are constants, and x is the variable being solved for. The solutions to a quadratic equation are the values of x that make the equation true.

Now, let's solve the quadratic equation $11x^2 - 1 = 0$ and understand it step by step using quadratic formula.

1. **Identify the coefficients:**

   In the equation $11x^2 - 1 = 0$,

   $$a=11, b=0, \text{ and } c=-1.$$

2. **Apply the quadratic formula:**

   The quadratic formula states that for an equation $ax^2 + bx + c = 0$, the solutions for x are given by:

   $$x = \frac{-b \pm \sqrt{b^2 - 4ac}}{2a}$$

   Plugging in the values a=11, b=0, and c=−1 into the quadratic formula, we get:

   $$x = \frac{-0 \pm \sqrt{0 - 4(11)(-1)}}{2(11)}$$

3. Simplify inside the square root:

$$0^2 - 4(11)(-1) = 0 - (-44) = 44$$

4. Plug in the simplified values:

$$x = \frac{\pm\sqrt{44}}{22}$$

5. Simplify the square root:

Since 44 is not a perfect square, we can write it as $\sqrt[2]{11}$

$$x = \frac{\pm\sqrt[2]{11}}{22}$$

6. Simplify further if possible:

We can simplify $\sqrt[2]{11}$ to $\sqrt{11}$ by canceling out the common factor:

$$x = \frac{\pm\sqrt{11}}{11}$$

7. Final solution:

So, the solutions to the equation are:

$$x = \frac{\sqrt{11}}{11} \text{ and } x = \frac{-\sqrt{11}}{11}$$

$$\text{or}$$

$$(x = 0.302, \text{ and } x = -0.302)$$

These are the roots of the quadratic equation. They represent the points where the graph of the quadratic equation intersects the x-axis.

Let's solve another equation:

$$-4p^2 + 6p - 6 = 0$$

$$p = \frac{-b \pm \sqrt{b^2 - 4ac}}{2a}$$

where $a = -4$, $b = 6$, and $c = -6$.

Let's plug these values into the quadratic formula:

$$p = \frac{-6 \pm \sqrt{6^2 - 4(-4)(-6)}}{2(-4)}$$

First, let's simplify inside the square root:

$$6^2 - 4\,(-4)\,(-6)$$

$$= 36 - 96 = -60$$

So, we have:

$$p = \frac{-6 \pm \sqrt{-60}}{-8}$$

We can simplify the square root of −60 by factoring out −1:

$$\sqrt{-60}$$

$$= \sqrt{-1 \times 60}$$

$$= \sqrt{-1} \times \sqrt{60}$$

$$= i\sqrt{60}$$

So, we have:

$$p = \frac{-6 \pm i\sqrt{60}}{-8}$$

Simplify:

$$\sqrt{60} \text{ to } \sqrt{4 \times 15} = 2\sqrt{15}$$

$$p = \frac{-6 \pm i \times 2\sqrt{15}}{-8}$$

Now, divide both the numerator and denominator by −2 to simplify:

$$p = \frac{3 \pm i\sqrt{15}}{4}$$

So, the solutions to the equation are:

$$p = \frac{3 + i\sqrt{15}}{4} \text{ and } p = \frac{3 - i\sqrt{15}}{4}$$

This equation -4p² + 6p - 6 = 0 has no real solutions.

When a quadratic equation has no real solutions, it means that the solutions are not real numbers, but rather complex numbers. In this case, the solutions involve the imaginary unit i because the discriminant ($b^2 - 4ac$) is negative, which results in taking the square root of a negative number when applying the quadratic formula.

In mathematics, such equations are said to have "no real roots" or "no real solutions." They are also sometimes referred to as having "complex roots" or "complex solutions." Complex numbers include a real part and an imaginary part, and they are often written in the form $a + bi$, where a and b are real numbers and i is the imaginary unit, defined as $i = \sqrt{-1}$.

Let's solve another equation:

$$12x^2 + 6x - 2 = 0$$

$$x = \frac{-b \pm \sqrt{b^2 - 4ac}}{2a}$$

where $a = 12$, $b = 6$, and $c = -2$.

Let's plug these values into the quadratic formula:

$$x = \frac{-6 \pm \sqrt{6^2 - 4(12)(-2)}}{2(12)}$$

First, let's simplify inside the square root:

$$6^2 - 4(12)(-2)$$

$$= 36 - (-96)$$

$$= 36 + 96$$

$$= 132$$

So, we have:

$$X = \frac{-6 \pm \sqrt{132}}{24}$$

Now, let's simplify the square root of 132:

$$X = \frac{-6 \pm \sqrt{4 \times 33}}{24}$$

$$X = \frac{-6 \pm 2\sqrt{33}}{24}$$

$$X = \frac{-6 \pm \sqrt{33}}{12}$$

So, the solutions to the equation are:

$$X = \frac{-6 + \sqrt{33}}{12} \text{ and } X = \frac{-6 - \sqrt{33}}{12}$$

or (x = 0.229, and x = -0.729)

Let's solve a quadratic equation where the right side is a number, instead of 0.

$$-8n^2 + 6n + 30 = 7$$

To solve the equation, we first need to bring all terms to one side to set the equation equal to zero:

$$-8n^2 + 6n + 30 - 7 = 0$$

Simplify:

$$-8n^2 + 6n + 23 = 0$$

Now, to solve for n, we can use the quadratic formula:

$$n = \frac{-b \pm \sqrt{b^2 - 4ac}}{2a}$$

where $a = -8$, $b = 6$, and $c = 23$.

Plugging these values into the formula, we get:

$$n = \frac{-6\pm\sqrt{6^2-4(-8)(23)}}{2(-8)}$$

$$n = \frac{-6\pm\sqrt{36+736}}{-16}$$

$$n = \frac{-6\pm\sqrt{772}}{-16}$$

Now, let's simplify the square root of 772. We can factor out 4:

$$\sqrt{772} = \sqrt{4 \times 193} = 2\sqrt{193}$$

So, our equation becomes:

$$n = \frac{-6\pm2\sqrt{193}}{-8}$$

So, the solutions to the equation are:

$$n = \frac{-3+\sqrt{193}}{-8} \text{ and } n = \frac{-3-\sqrt{193}}{-8}$$

or

(n = -1.362, and n = 2.112)

Polynomials

A polynomial is an algebraic expression consisting of one or more terms, where each term is a constant, a variable, or a product of constants and variables raised to whole number exponents.

Examples of polynomials include:

- $(7v^2 + 2v^4) + (8v^2 + 4v^4)$
- $(2v + 4v^2 + 2) - (5v - 4v^4 - 6v^2)$
- $(7x - 5\,y)(2x - 6\,y)$
- $(6x^2 + 4xy + 6\,y^2)(8x^2 + 3xy + 3\,y^2)$
- $\dfrac{2x^3 + 8x^2 + 2x}{2x^2}$

Operations on Polynomials

Addition of Polynomials:

- To add polynomials, simply combine like terms.
- Like terms are terms that have the same variable(s) raised to the same power(s).
- For example, to add $3x^2 + 2x$ and $5x^2 - 7x$, group the like terms: $3x^2 + 5x^2$ and $2x - 7x$, then add each group separately.

Subtraction of Polynomials:

- To subtract polynomials, distribute the negative sign and then add.
- For example, to subtract $x^2 - 2x$ from $4x^2 + 3x$, distribute the negative sign to each term in the second polynomial: $-(x^2 - 2x)$, then add each term separately.

<u>Multiplication of Polynomials:</u>

- To multiply polynomials, use the distributive property and then combine like terms.

- For example, to multiply $(x + 2)(3x - 4)$, distribute each term in the first polynomial to each term in the second polynomial, then combine like terms.

<u>Division of Polynomials:</u>

- Division of polynomials involves dividing one polynomial by another. It can be done using long division or synthetic division.

Let's solve the expression:
$$(7x^2 - 7x) - (x - 2x^2)$$

Step 1: Distribute the Negative Sign:

Distribute the negative sign in the second polynomial:
$$(7x^2 - 7x) - x + 2x^2$$

Step 2: Combine Like Terms:
$$(7x^2 + 2x^2) + (-7x - x)$$

Step 3: Perform addition and subtraction of coefficients:
$$9x^2 - 8x$$

Let's perform the multiplication of polynomials:
$$(5u + 2v)(8u^2 - uv - 3v^2)$$

We can distribute each term in the first polynomial $(5u+2v)$ to every term in the second polynomial $(8u2 - uv - 3v2)$.

1. Multiply $5u$ by each term in the second polynomial:
$$5u \cdot 8u^2 = 40u^3$$
$$5u \cdot (-uv) = -5u^2v$$
$$5u \cdot (-3v^2) = -15uv^2$$

2. Multiply $2v$ by each term in the second polynomial:

$$2v \cdot 8u^2 = 16u^2v$$

$$2v \cdot (-uv) = -2uv^2$$

$$2v \cdot (-3v^2) = -6v^3$$

Combine the like terms:

$$40u^3 - 5u^2v - 15uv^2 + 16u^2v - 2uv^2 - 6v^3$$

Combine the like terms involving u and v.

$$40u^3 + (16u^2v - 5u^2v) + (-15uv^2 - 2uv^2) - 6v^3$$

$$40u^3 + 11u^2v - 17uv^2 - 6v^3$$

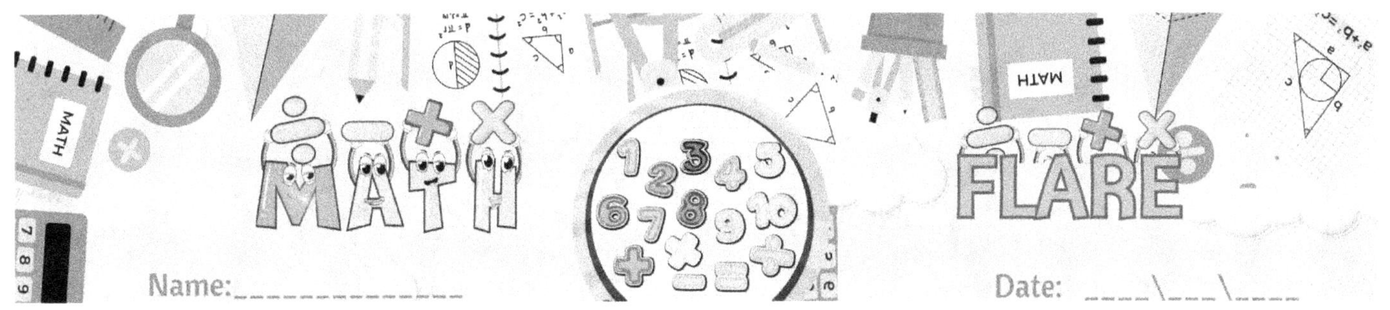

Equations (One Side)
Solve for the variable.

1. $20 - 5k = 0$

2. $m \times 5 = 35$

3. $8 \times x = 80$

4. $54 \div k = 9$

5. $7 - z = 5$

6. $z - 3 = 5$

7. $y \times 8 = 8$

8. $4x + 9 = 37$

9. $7 - z = 1$

10. $y + 7 = 14$

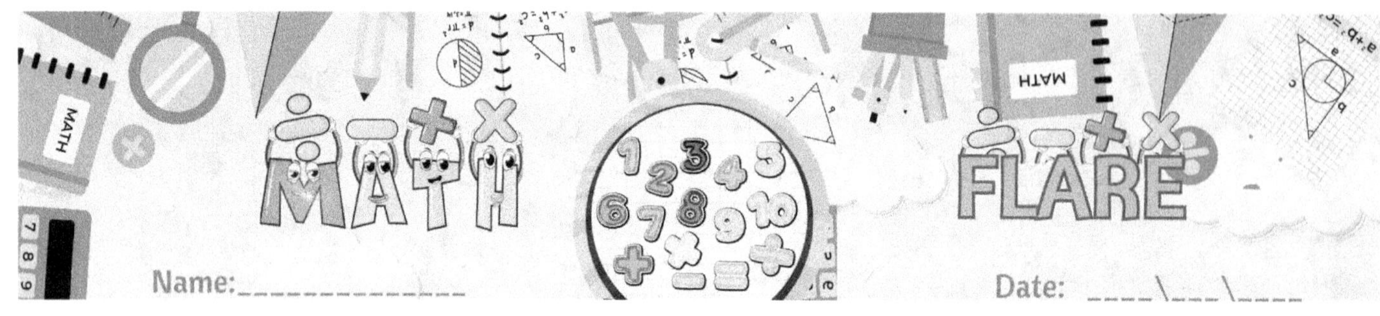

11. $m - 6 = 2$

12. $4 - x = 1$

13. $x + 1 = 11$

14. $x + 5 = 8$

15. $10 + 7z = 80$

16. $y \times 3 = 9$

17. $6 + m = 9$

18. $k \div 9 = 1$

19. $z - 1 = 4$

20. $m \times 9 = 18$

21. $6 \times m = 60$

22. $10 + 7y = 45$

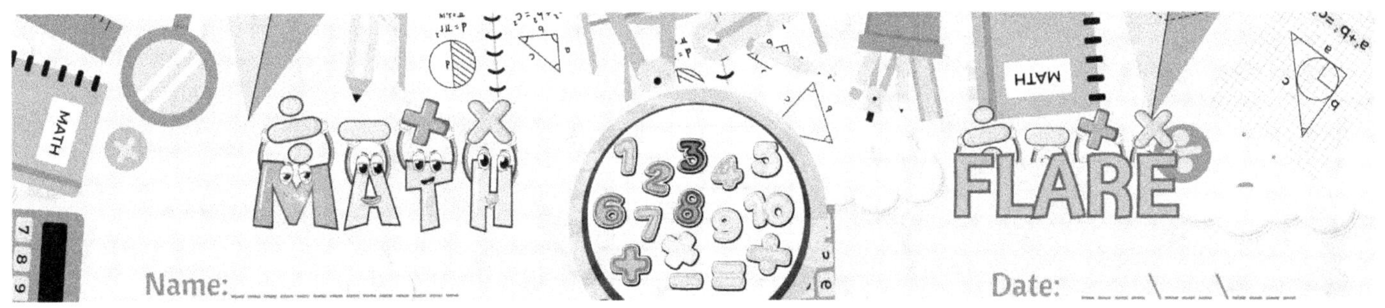

23. $1 \div m = 1$

24. $7 + y = 17$

25. $7 - k = 3$

26. $10 - m = 9$

27. $8 + m = 16$

28. $8 - z = 1$

29. $10 \times m = 60$

30. $4 + 8x = 76$

31. $3 \times m = 12$

32. $8 + k = 17$

33. $6 - z = 4$

34. $6 - k = 2$

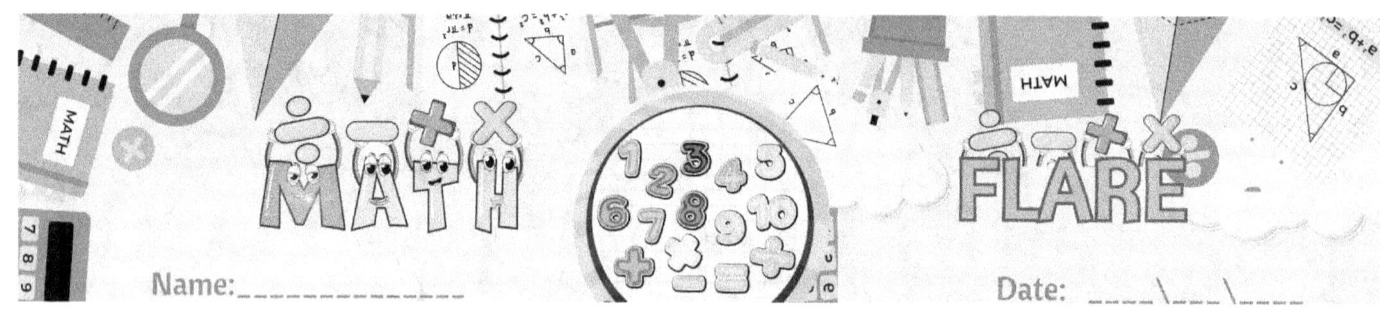

35. $63 \div z = 7$

36. $10 - y = 2$

37. $z + 8 = 12$

38. $7z + 3 = 17$

39. $x + 6 = 12$

40. $x - 5 = 4$

41. $7 - z = 5$

42. $x + 9 = 12$

43. $4 + m = 11$

44. $2 \times m = 8$

45. $m + 3 = 4$

46. $7 + 8z = 71$

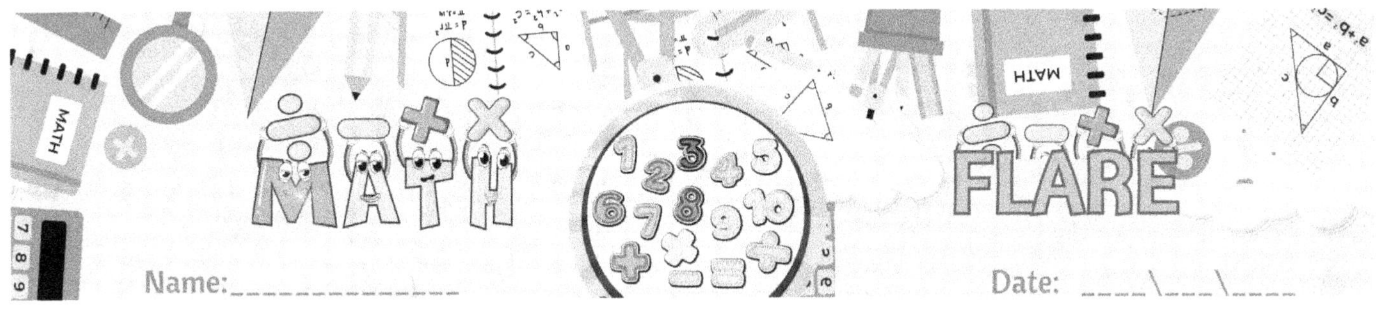

47. $k - 1 = 6$

48. $8 + x = 14$

49. $30 \div k = 6$

50. $k \div 6 = 4$

51. $6 \times y = 42$

52. $21 - 4m = 5$

53. $8 - 1y = 6$

54. $30 \div x = 5$

55. $2k - 4 = 12$

56. $20 \div x = 4$

57. $10 + z = 12$

58. $z - 1 = 4$

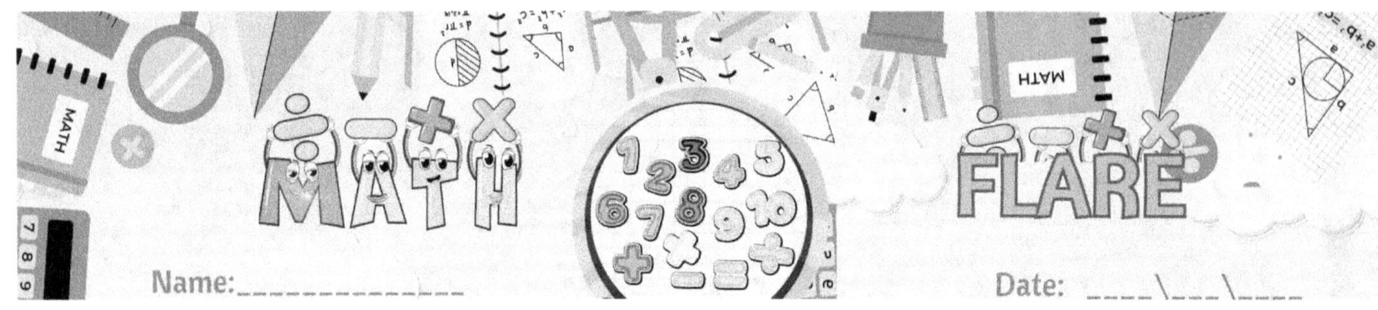

59. $3 + k = 8$

60. $10x + 5 = 25$

61. $y + 5 = 13$

62. $y \times 2 = 10$

63. $k \div 1 = 6$

64. $9 + x = 17$

65. $m + 2 = 12$

66. $17 - 10m = 7$

67. $3y - 6 = 0$

68. $27 \div m = 3$

69. $x - 3 = 3$

70. $k - 2 = 1$

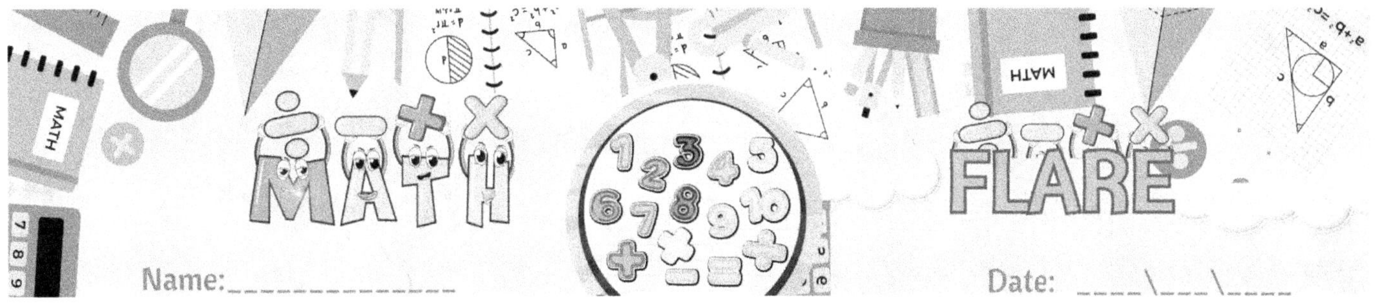

Name:___________________ Date: ____________

71. $9z - 2 = 7$

72. $m \times 4 = 16$

73. $36 \div y = 9$

74. $7 + x = 12$

75. $10m - 3 = 77$

76. $y - 5 = 0$

77. $m \div 5 = 4$

78. $4 + k = 14$

79. $m + 9 = 19$

80. $6 \times m = 54$

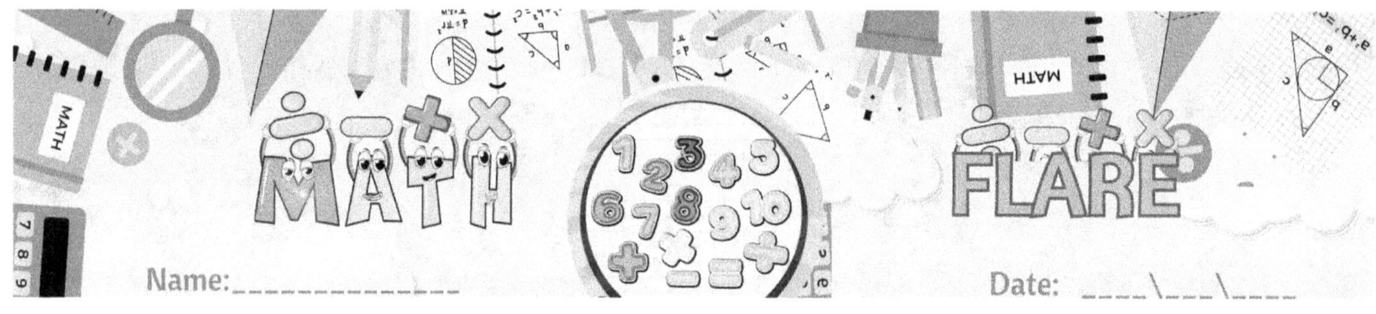

Name:________________   Date: ____________

Equations (Two Sides)
Solve for the variable.

81. $35 - y = 6y$

82. $56 + y = 8y$

83. $5z + 9 = 51 - z$

84. $6 - z = 2z$

85. $4 + x = 3 + 2x$

86. $1 + 6z + 9 = 13 + z + 7$

87. $3 + 2y = 12 - y$

88. $4y = 25 - y$

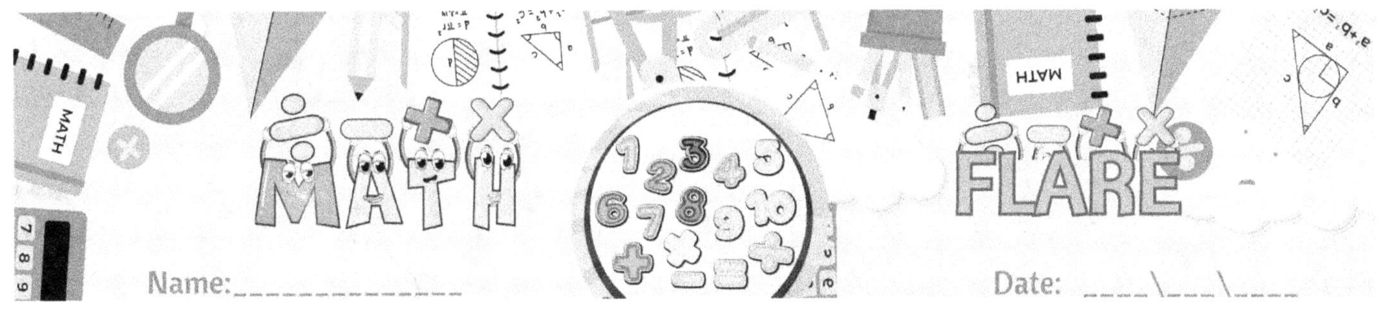

Name:_________________ Date: ____________

89. $9 + 2z + 5 = 23 - z$

90. $20 - y + 13 = 8 + 2y + 7$

91. $4 + 2z + 2 = 33 - z$

92. $3 + 3k = 21 + k$

93. $5k = 12 - k$

94. $16 - k = 4 + 5k$

95. $35 + x = 6x$

96. $9 - z = 2z$

97. $6 + 2m + 2 = 20 + m + -5$

98. $22 + y = 4y + 1$

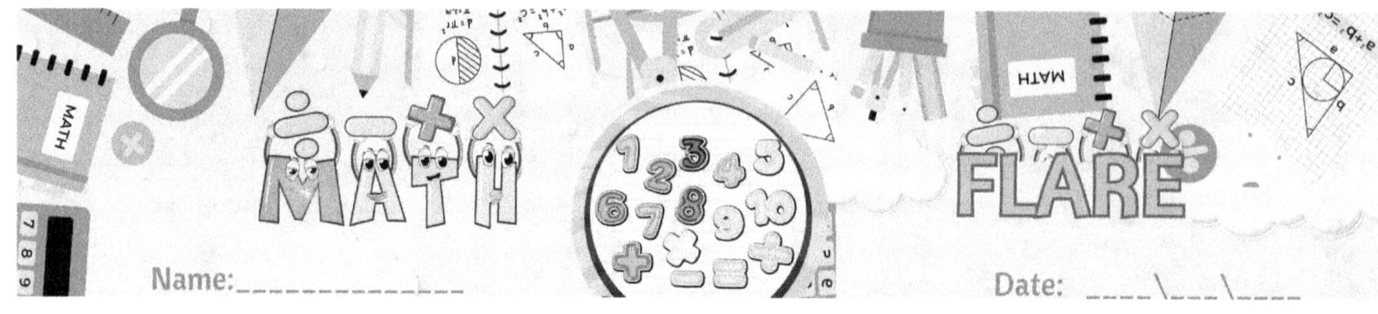

99. $5 + 4x + 6 = 29 + x$

100. $8y + 3 = 6y + 11$

101. $3z = 12 + z$

102. $72 - x = 7 + 8x + 2$

103. $6 + 2k = 9 - k$

104. $1 + 6z = 57 - z$

105. $24 + z = 4z$

106. $54 + 2z = 7z + 9$

107. $46 - 6x = 7x + 7$

108. $8x + 2 = 17 - 7x$

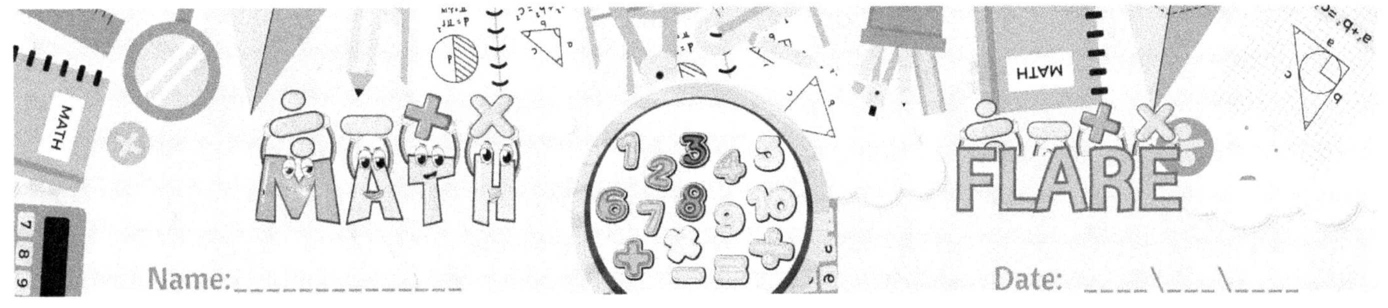

109. $4k + 6 = 33 + k$

110. $71 + k = 9 + 8k + 6$

111. $16 - x = 6 + 5x + 4$

112. $3 + m = 4m$

113. $3k = 14 + k$

114. $46 - 4z = 7z + 2$

115. $79 - 3z = 5z + 7$

116. $3y + 2 = 10 - y$

117. $5 + 7m = 37 - m$

118. $3z + 9 = 15 + z$

119. $81 - 3k = 9 + 9k$

120. $35 + x + -2 = 7 + 7x + 2$

121. $8 + 3x = 14 + x$

122. $21 - 6z = 8z + 7$

123. $4z + 8 = 32 + z$

124. $34 - 2k = 4 + 3k$

125. $9 + 7k + 9 = 26 - k$

126. $49 + k = 8k$

127. $29 + z = 4 + 4z + 7$

128. $3x = 8 - x$

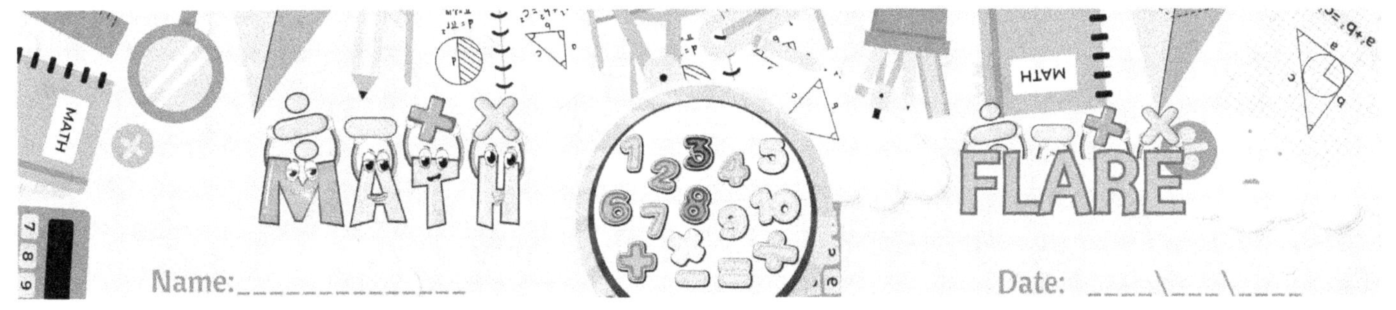

129. $10 - k + 4 = 4 + 2k + 1$

130. $18 + x = 3x$

131. $8 + 6k = 40 - 2k$

132. $8z + 1 = 10 - z$

133. $63 - m = 6m$

134. $3k = 18 + k$

135. $25 + x = 6x$

136. $9k + 2 = 87 - 8k$

137. $43 + y + 1 = 9 + 5y + 3$

138. $6 - k = 2k$

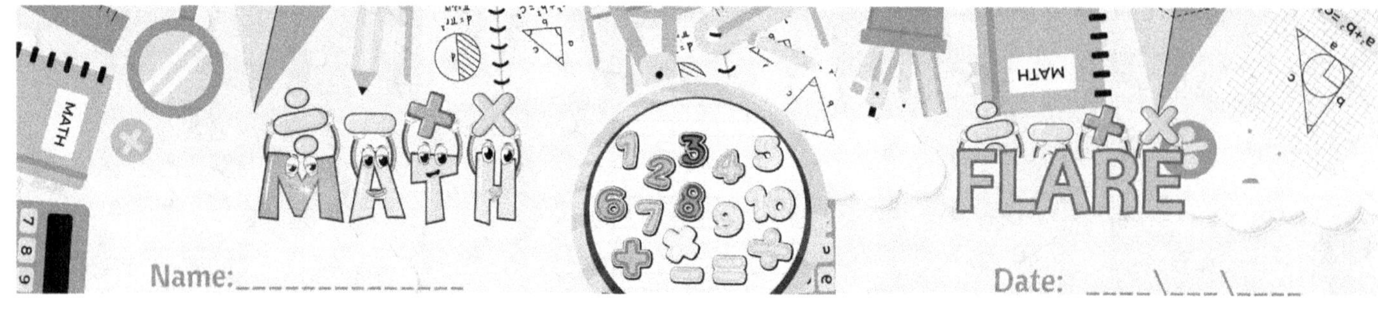

139. $2k = 21 - k$

140. $10 + y = 2 + 4y + 5$

141. $5 + 3m = 13 - m$

142. $6 + m = 3m$

143. $86 - 7x = 9x + 6$

144. $7 + 3y = 15 - y$

145. $18 + 5k = 6 + 9k$

146. $45 - x + 9 = 4 + 8x + 5$

147. $3 + 6z = 38 - z$

148. $25 + m = 4 + 4m$

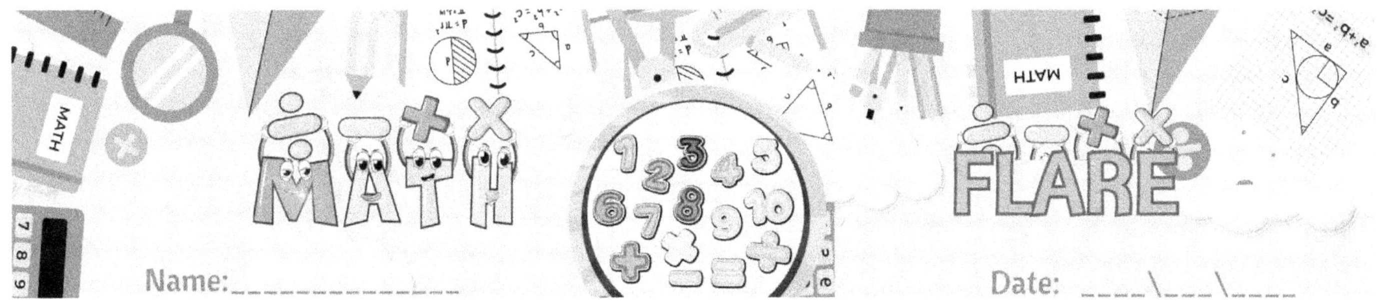

Name:________________   Date: ______________

149. $2k = 4 + k$

150. $6y = 63 - y$

151. $4 + 8x = 6x + 20$

152. $2 + 6x + 9 = 50 + x + 1$

153. $21 + y = 6y + 1$

154. $4z + 1 = 31 - z$

155. $1 + 8k + 6 = 54 - k + 7$

156. $37 + z = 9 + 8z$

157. $6y = 42 - y$

158. $56 - z = 6z$

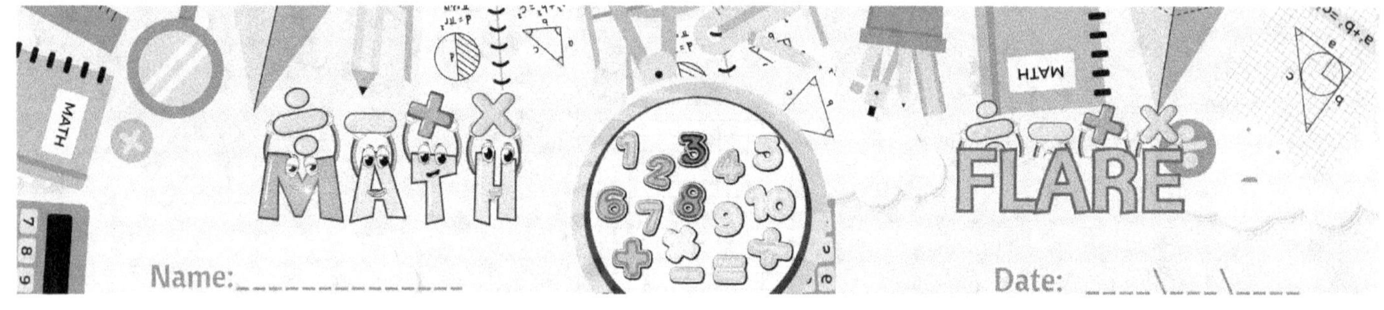

159. $4 + 2y + 4 = 23 - y$

160. $4 + z = 2z$

161. $17 - z + 7 = 7 + 2z + 2$

162. $44 - z = 8 + 8z$

163. $43 - 5m = 9m + 1$

164. $5 + 8x + 7 = 63 - x + 12$

165. $2 + 9z = 14 + 5z$

166. $8 + 2y = 3 + 3y$

167. $9 + 9k = 8k + 15$

168. $5 + 2k + 4 = 12 - k$

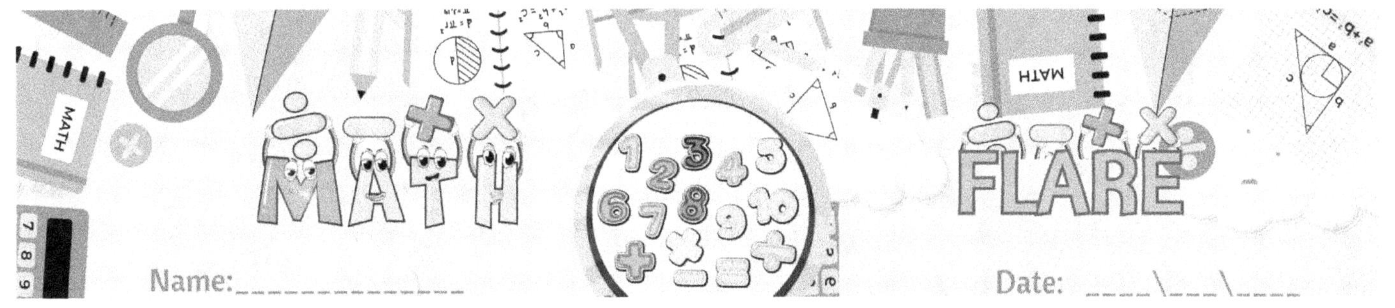

169. $42 - x = 5 + 7x + 5$

170. $43 - 2y = 3 + 6y$

171. $9 + 3z = 13 + z$

172. $8m = 63 + m$

173. $1 + 7z = 3 + 5z$

174. $20 - 7x = 5 + 8x$

175. $22 - m = 3 + 6m + 5$

176. $13 - m = 5m + 1$

177. $1 + 3m + 4 = 9 + m$

178. $45 + k = 6k + 5$

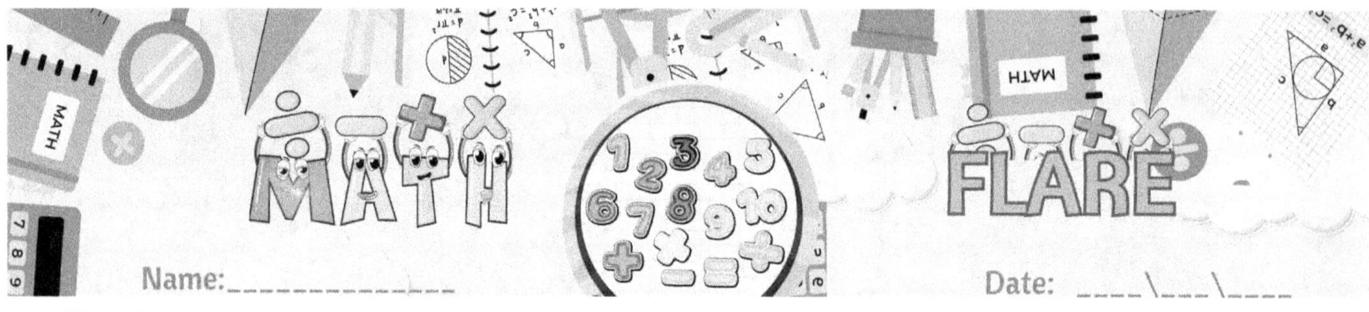

Evaluating Equations

Evaluate each expression when: x = 2

179. $7x + 5x + 9x =$

180. $9 + 3x =$

181. $4 + x =$

182. $3 + 10x =$

183. $3 + x =$

184. $8(2 - x) =$

185. $1 + x =$

186. $6(9 - x) =$

187. $9(4 - x) =$

188. $5x + 5x - 6 =$

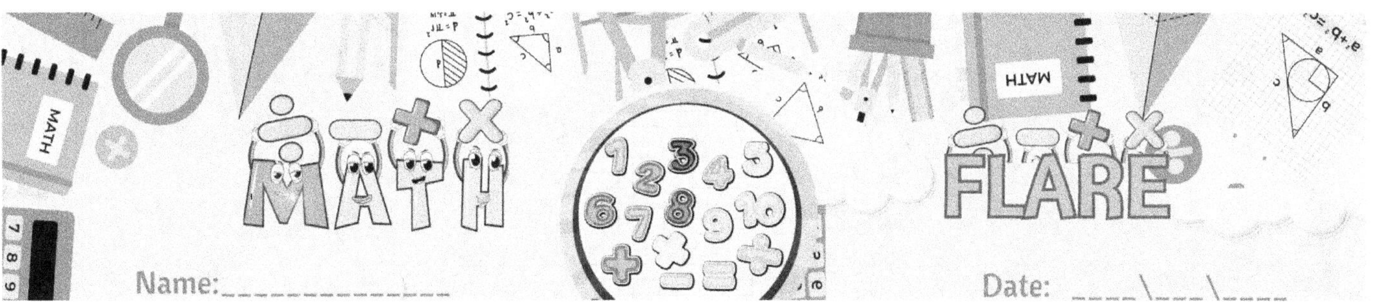

Evaluating Equations
Evaluate each expression when: x = 4

189. x – 2 =

190. 8 + x =

191. 5x + 4 =

192. x – 3 =

193. x – 10 =

194. 2 – x =

195. 5(7 – x) =

196. x + 4 + 10x =

197. 3x + 6 =

198. 3 + 5x =

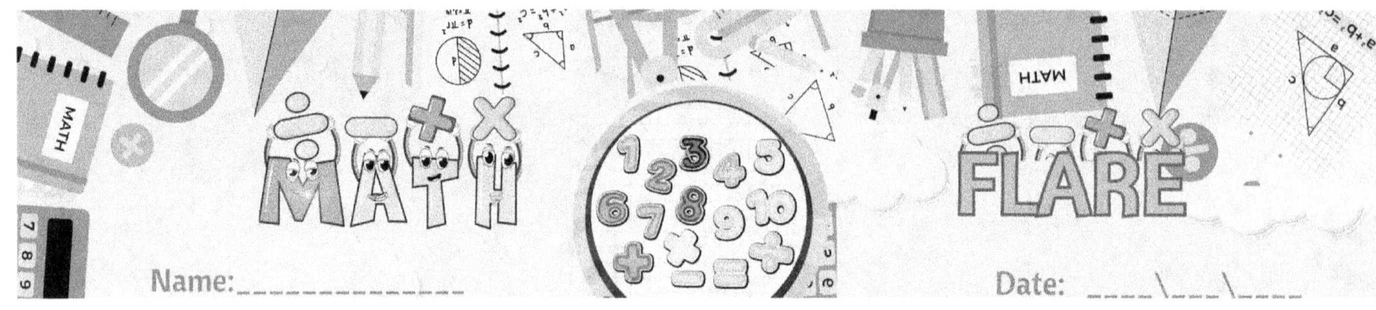

Evaluating Equations

Evaluate each expression when: x = 3

199. $1 + x =$

200. $8x + 5 =$

201. $9 + x =$

202. $4x - 10 =$

203. $10x - x =$

204. $1 - x =$

205. $10x - 7 =$

206. $2 + 5x =$

207. $5(8 + x) =$

208. $x - 2 =$

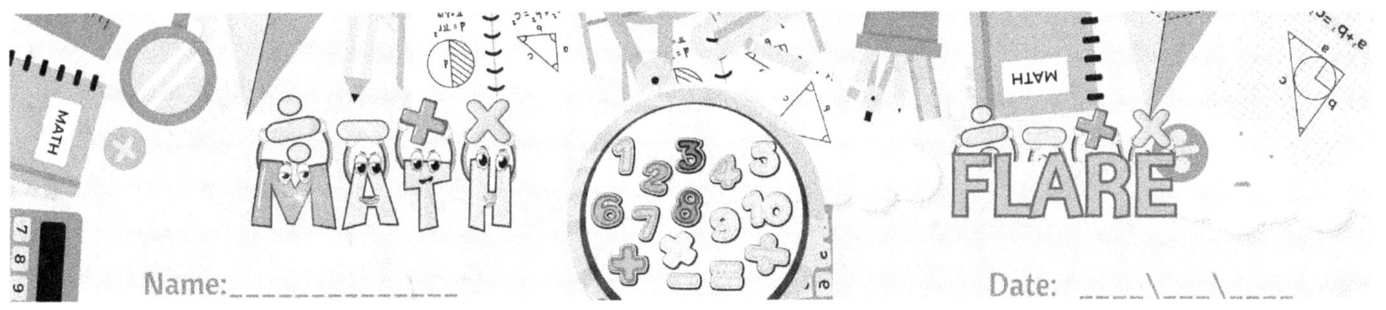

Name:_______________ Date: ____________

Evaluating Equations

Evaluate each expression when: x = 3

209. $2 + x =$

210. $6 + 6x =$

211. $x + 8 =$

212. $5x - 2 =$

213. $x + 8 =$

214. $9(4 - x) =$

215. $x + 9 + 8x =$

216. $x + 1 =$

217. $4(7 - x) =$

218. $x + 3 =$

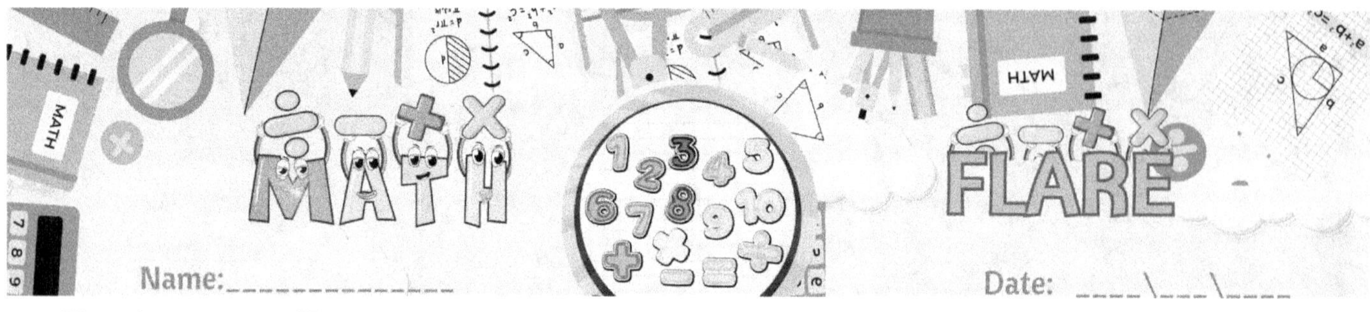

Evaluating Equations

Evaluate each expression when: x = 1

219. $7x + 2 =$

220. $x + 5 =$

221. $8x - 9 =$

222. $1(8 + x) =$

223. $4(5 + x) =$

224. $10 + 8x =$

225. $x + 8 =$

226. $3x + 7 =$

227. $10(8 + x) =$

228. $3 - x =$

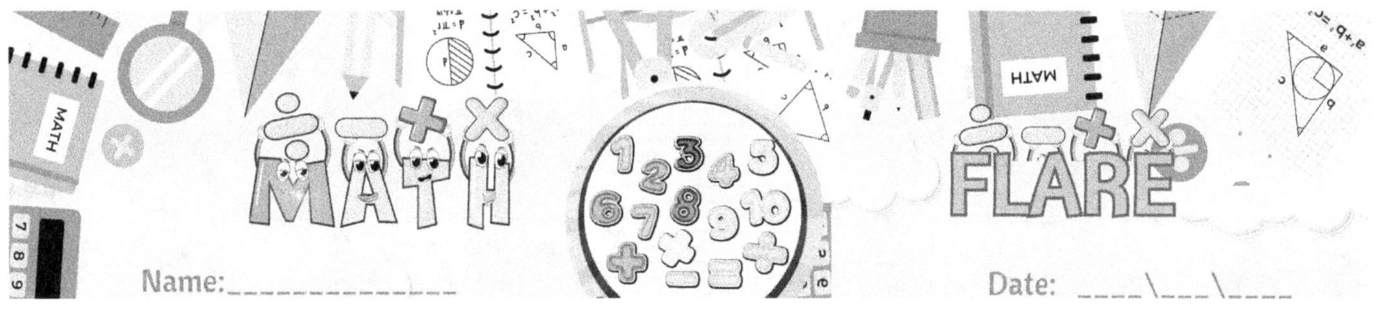

Name:_______________   Date: ____________

Evaluating Equations

Evaluate each expression when: x = 4

229. $2(6 - x) =$

230. $2x + 2 =$

231. $2x - 2 =$

232. $1(7 - x) =$

233. $x - 10 =$

234. $2(10 + x) =$

235. $10 + 3x =$

236. $10(2 - x) =$

237. $4x - x =$

238. $x - x =$

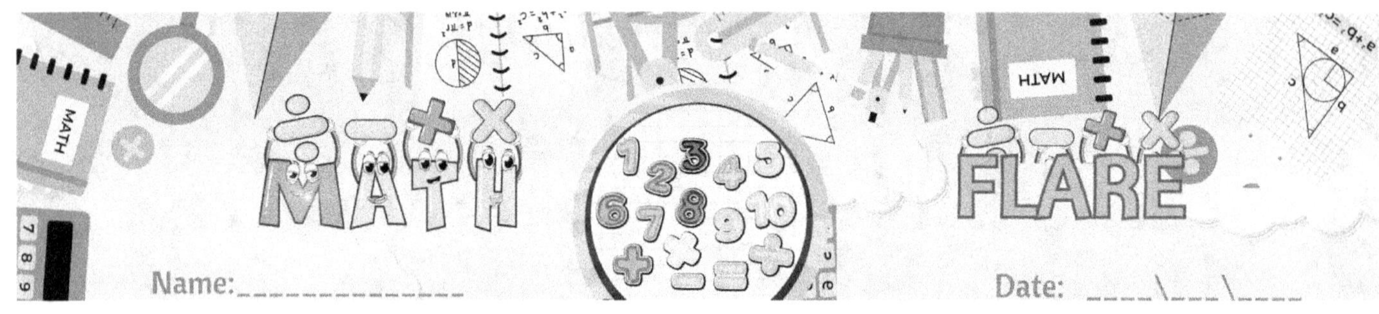

Name:_________________________

Date: _____________

Evaluating Equations

Evaluate each expression when: $x = 4$

239. $5x + 1 =$

240. $1 + x =$

241. $x + 3 + 6x =$

242. $4(3 - x) =$

243. $10(9 + x) =$

244. $7(6 - x) =$

245. $7 + x =$

246. $3x + 8 =$

247. $x + 8 =$

248. $9x + 2 =$

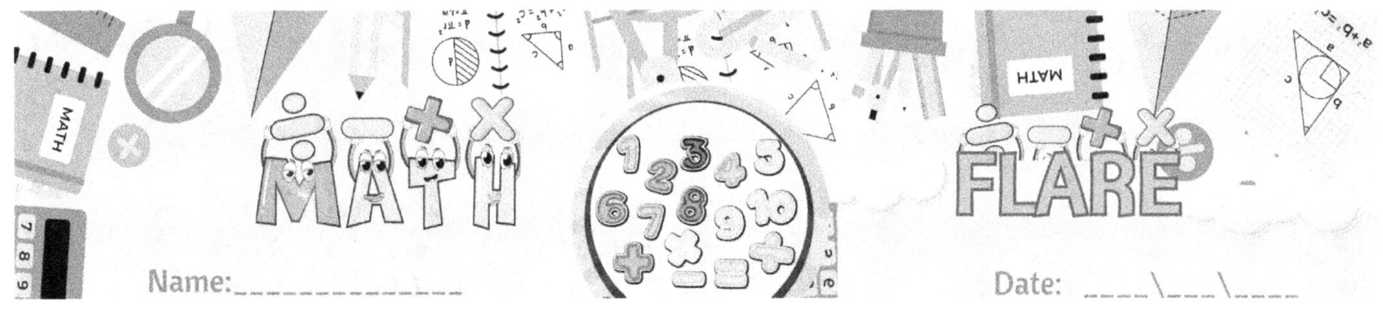

Solving Inequalities

249.

$$8 > x - 5$$

250.

$$-6 > z + -9$$

251.

$$2\,m > -5$$

252.

$$\frac{y}{-3} \geq 2$$

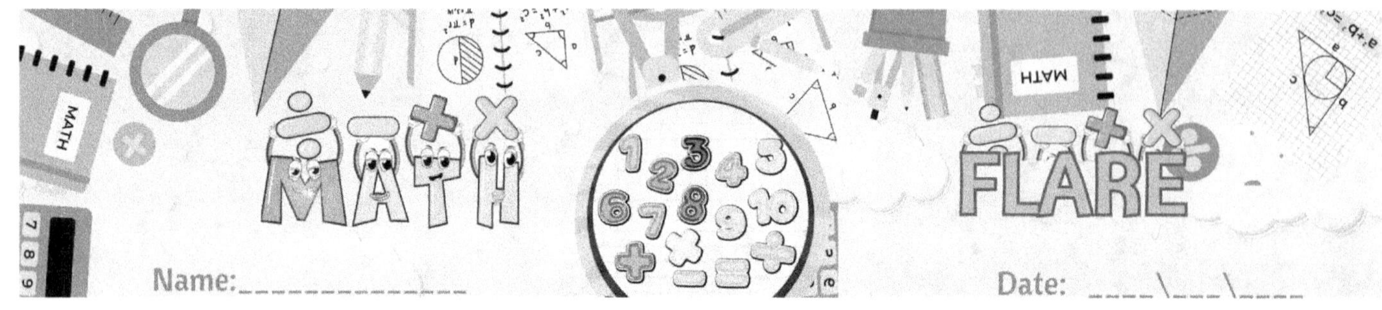

253.

$$6 - x < 9$$

254.

$$k + 2 \leq 5$$

255.

$$\frac{z}{-2} \leq -9$$

256.

$$-2 < 4y$$

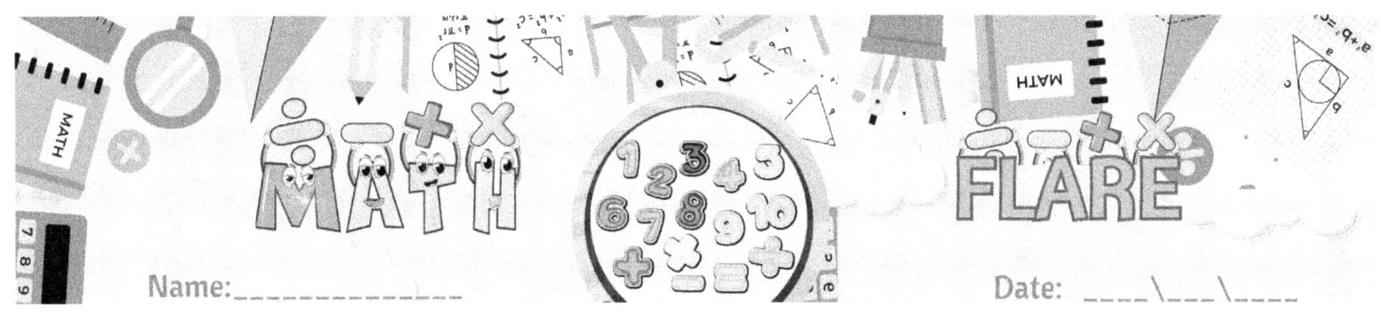

257.
$$-7 > x + 1$$

258.
$$\frac{z}{8} \leq 5$$

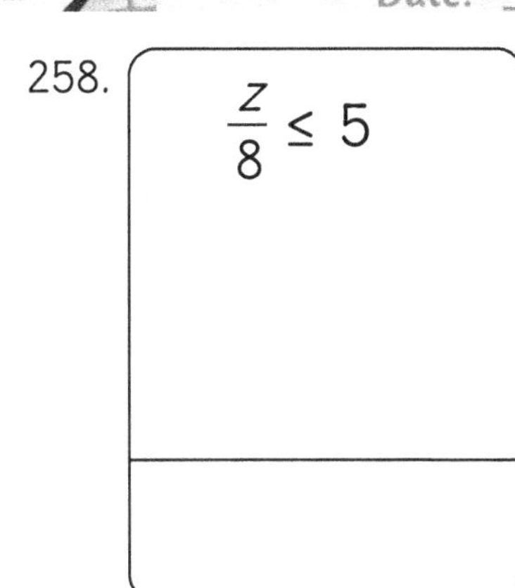

259.
$$k - 7 < 9$$

260.
$$10 \geq -8\,m$$

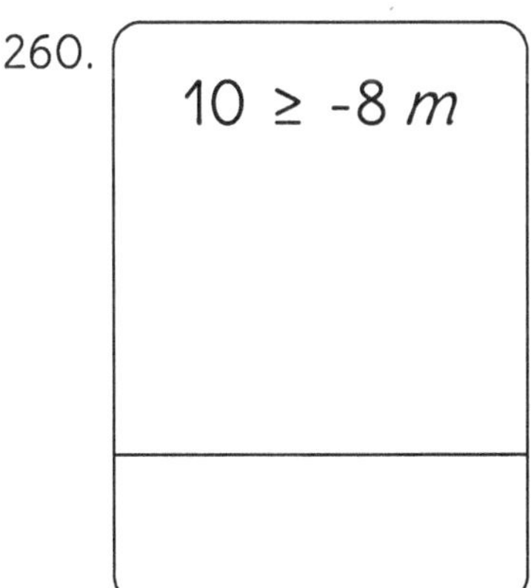

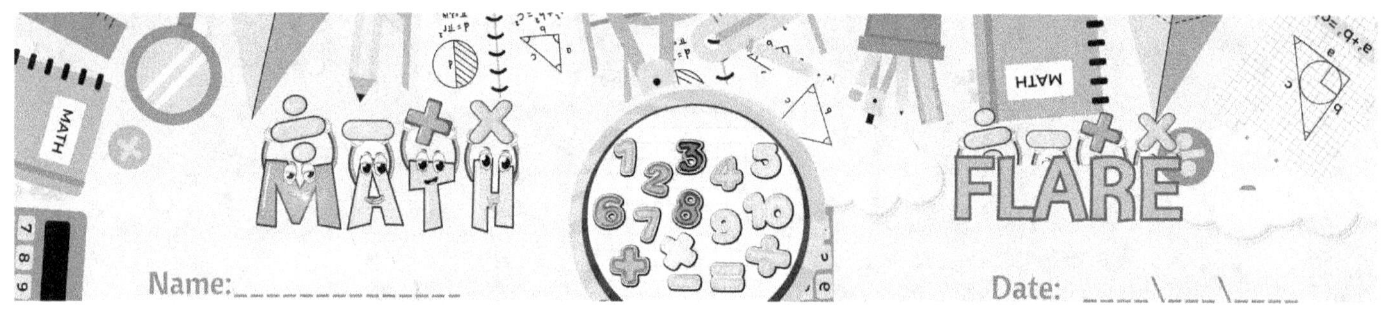

Name:_______________ Date: _______________

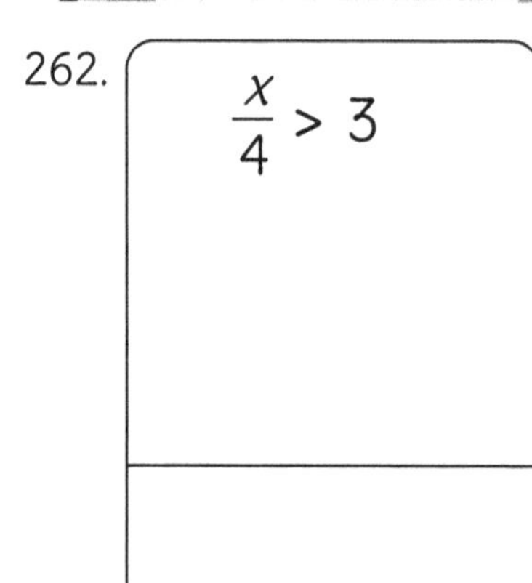

261.

$$-6\,z > 2$$

262.

$$\frac{x}{4} > 3$$

263.

$$-4 + k \geq 8$$

264.

$$7 > 3 - y$$

265.
$$-1 \geq -5 - k$$

266. 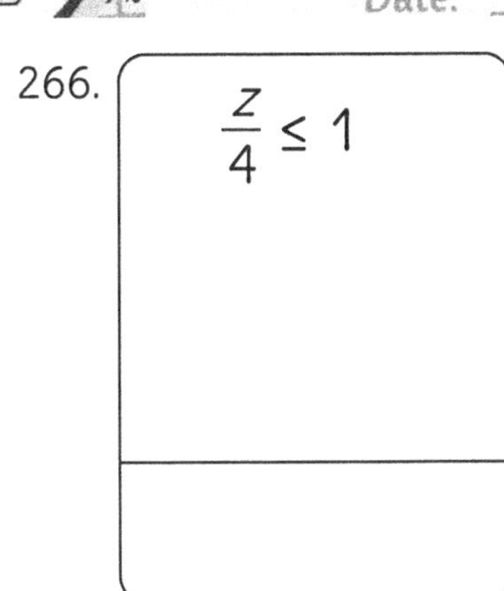
$$\frac{z}{4} \leq 1$$

267.
$$-5 < -2 + k$$

268.
$$8 \leq 6z$$

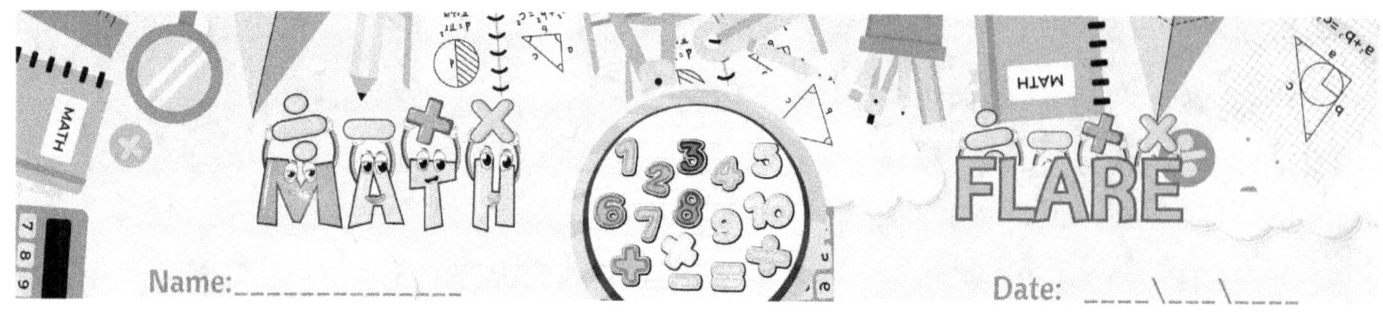

269.

$$-6\,y \leq 10$$

270.

$$\frac{y}{-3} \leq 6$$

271.

$$k + 3 \geq 5$$

272.

$$x - -8 < -2$$

273. $y + -1 > -10$

274. $\dfrac{k}{-7} \geq -9$

275. $-3 > -7 - y$

276. $-12 < 12\,k$

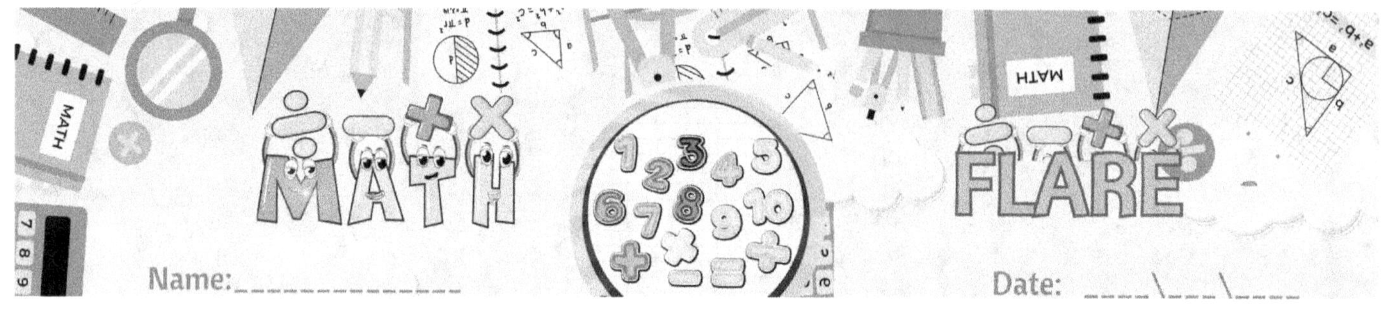

277.

$$10 \leq 6\,m$$

278.

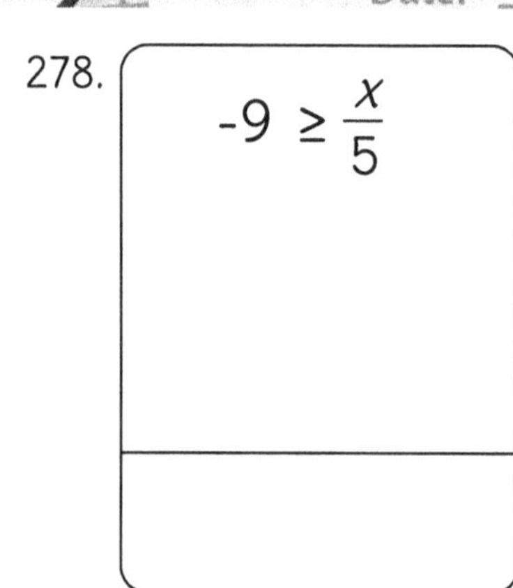

$$-9 \geq \frac{x}{5}$$

279.

$$4 + m \geq 6$$

280.

$$x - 1 \leq 8$$

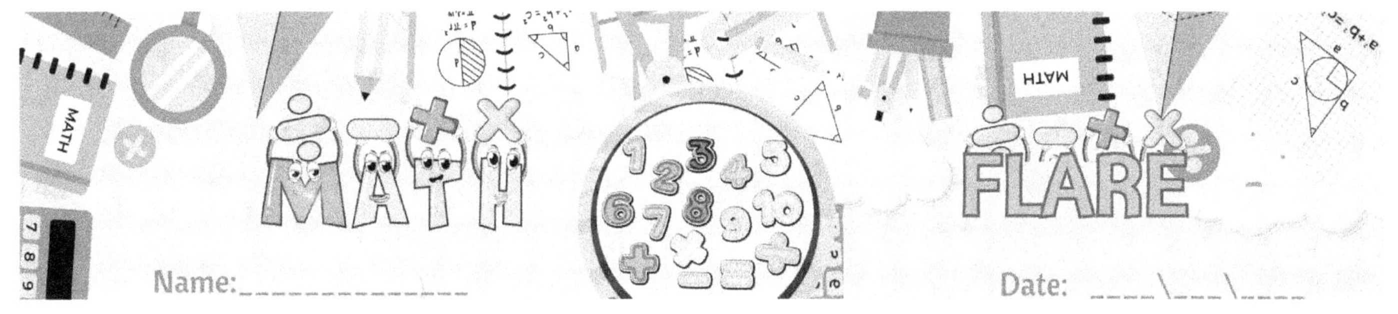

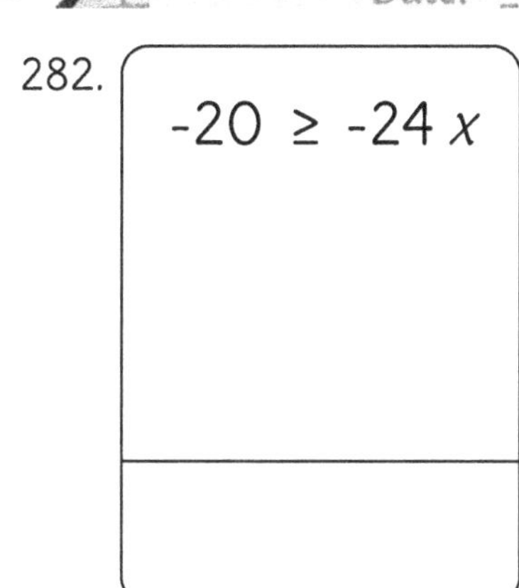

281.

$$-7 - y \geq -1$$

282.

$$-20 \geq -24x$$

283.

$$\frac{k}{5} < -7$$

284.

$$-4 \geq 2 + m$$

Name:_________________   Date: ________________

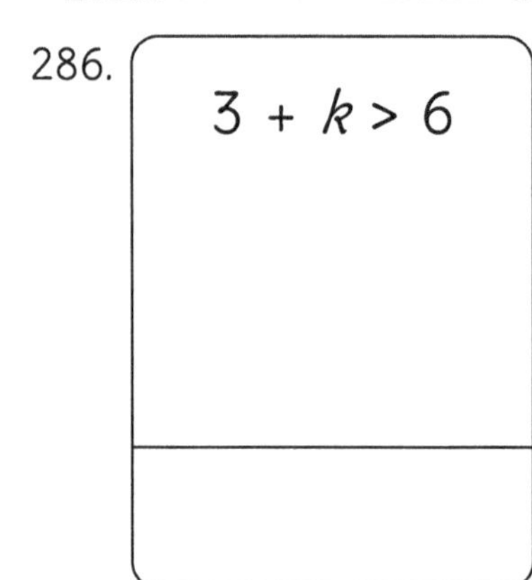

285.

$$-5 \leq \frac{y}{1}$$

286.

$$3 + k > 6$$

287.

$$9 \leq k - -8$$

288.

$$-9\,k > -18$$

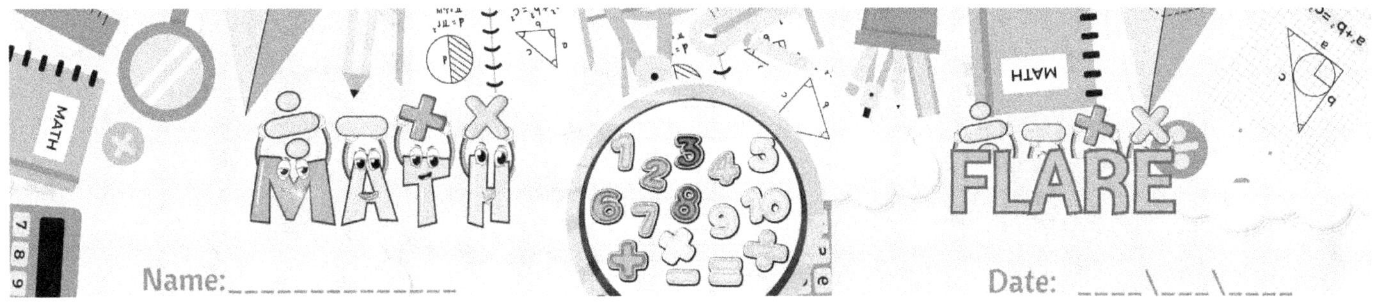

Verbal Algebra

289. One number is eight times another. Their sum is 81. Find the numbers.

290. Three times a number is 6. What is the number?

291. The quotient of a number and nine is 5. Find the number.

292. The product of three and a number is 15. What is the number?

293. A number decreased by 1 is 4. Find the number.

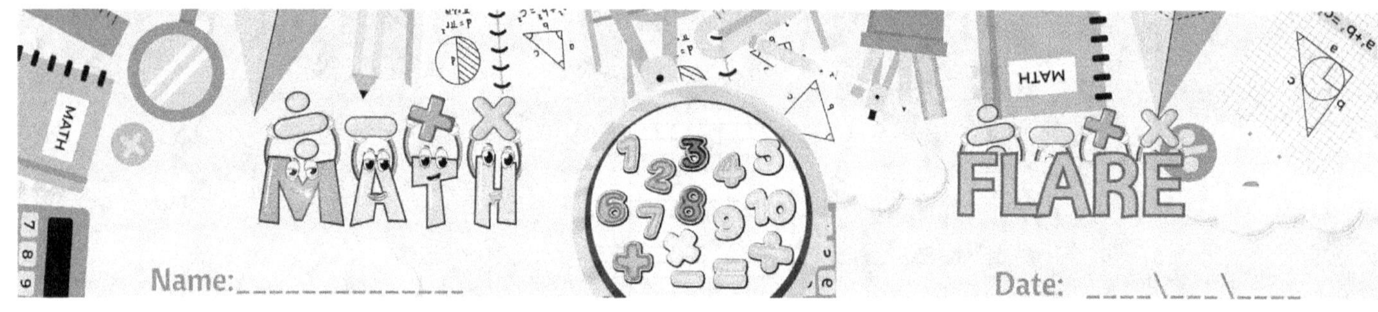

294. One less than six times a number is 29. Find the number.

295. Two-thirds of a number is 0. Find the number.

296. Twice a number is 8. What is the number?

297. The quotient of a number and five is 2. Find the number.

298. When a number is divided by two, the result is 6. What is the number?

299. The product of two and a number is 14. What is the number?

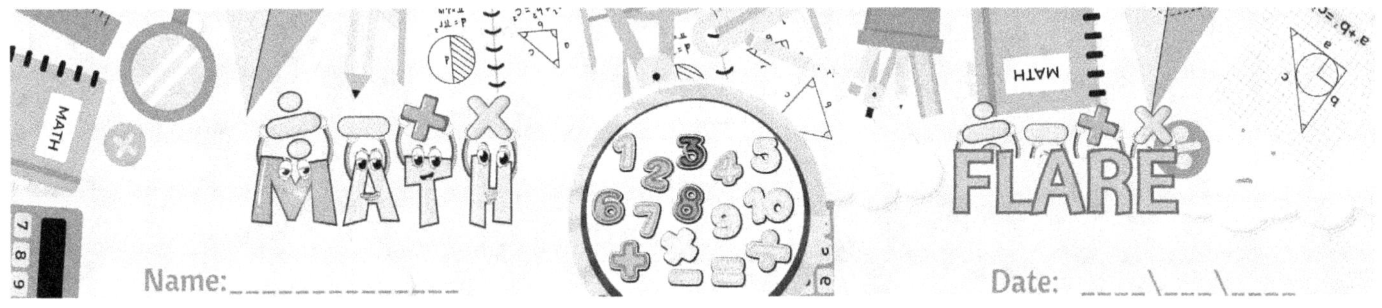

300. The sum of two consecutive numbers is 15. What are the numbers?

301. A number decreased by 6 is 8. Find the number.

302. One-third of a number is 1. Find the number.

303. The quotient of a number and seven is 3. Find the number.

304. One less than four times a number is 23. Find the number.

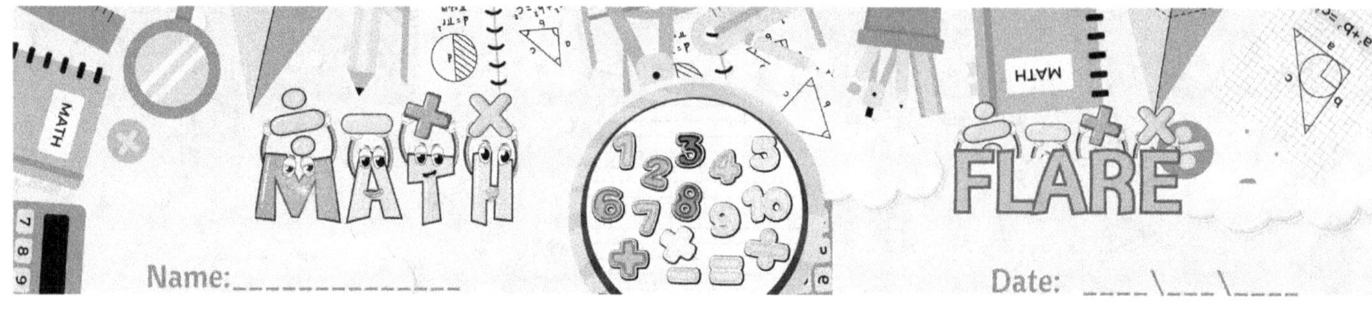

305.   One number is six times another. Their sum is 42. Find the numbers.

306.   Twice a number is 6. What is the number?

307.   A number decreased by 7 is 9. Find the number.

308.   Seven less than a number is 5. Find the number.

309.   A number decreased by 1 is 1. Find the number.

310.   Ten times a number is 0. What is the number?

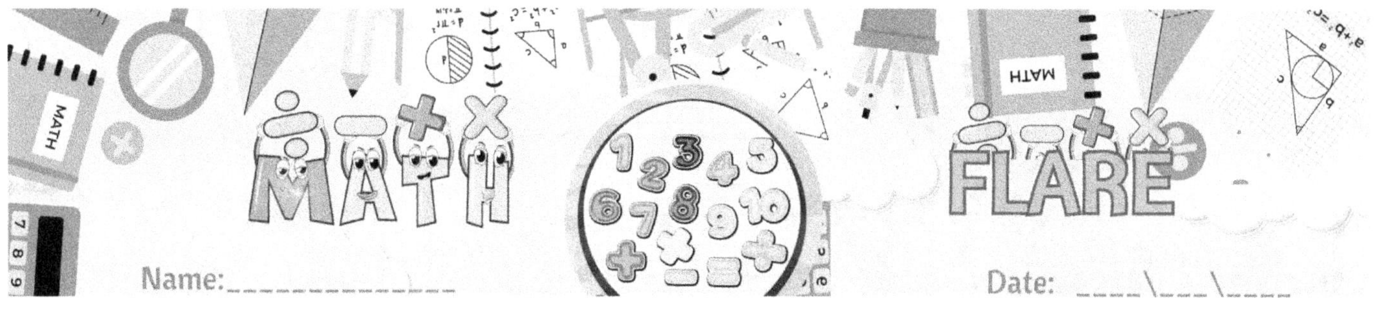

311. The sum of a number and nine is 17. Find the number.

312. Four more than a number is 10. What is the number?

313. A number decreased by 1 is 9. Find the number.

314. When a number is divided by seven, the result is 1. What is the number?

315. Nine less than a number is 2. Find the number.

316. When a number is divided by ten, the result is 5. What is the number?

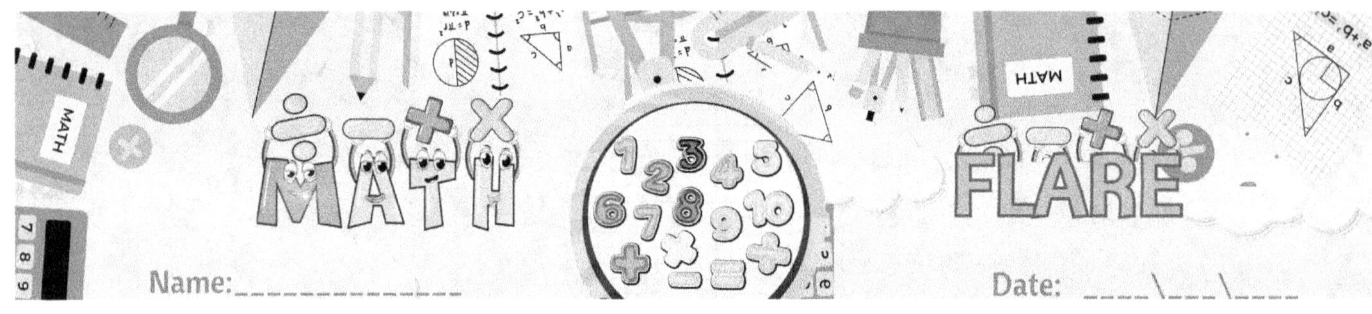

317. One number is five times another. Their sum is 6. Find the numbers.

318. The quotient of a number and ten is 2. Find the number.

319. Two more than a number is 10. What is the number?

320. When a number is divided by eight, the result is 2. What is the number?

321. Nine more than a number is 12. What is the number?

322. Four less than a number is 6. Find the number.

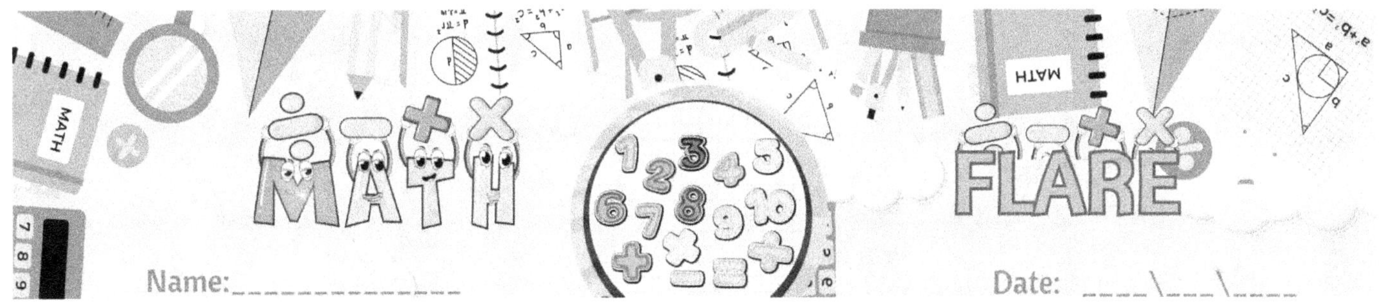

323. One less than three times a number is 20. Find the number.

324. The sum of a number and three is 9. Find the number.

325. Four more than a number is 5. What is the number?

326. The sum of a number and two is 6. Find the number.

327. One less than eight times a number is 63. Find the number.

328. Six less than a number is 3. Find the number.

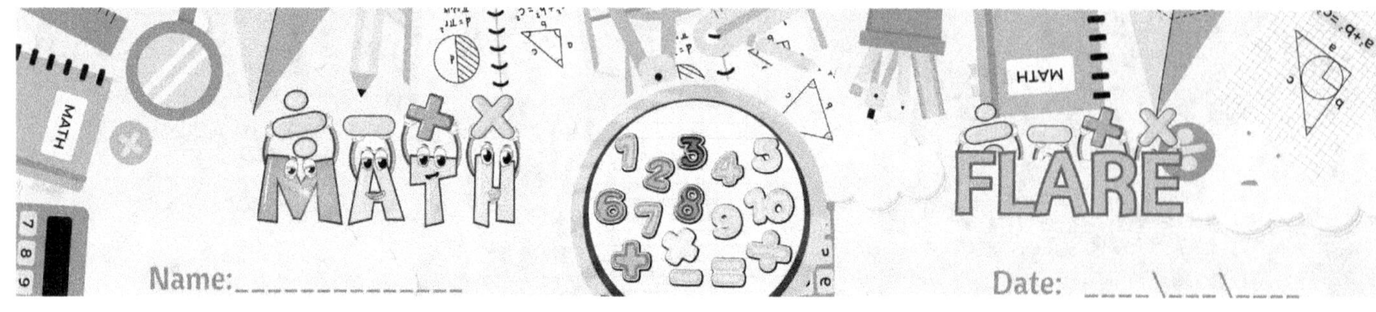

Standard Linear Equations

1. 2x + 4 = -6

2. -5x + -5 = 0

3. 1x + 5 = 15

4. -3x + -2 = 19

5. 3x + -3 = -21

6. -8x + -1 = -81

7. -2x + -5 = 15

8. 3x + -7 = -22

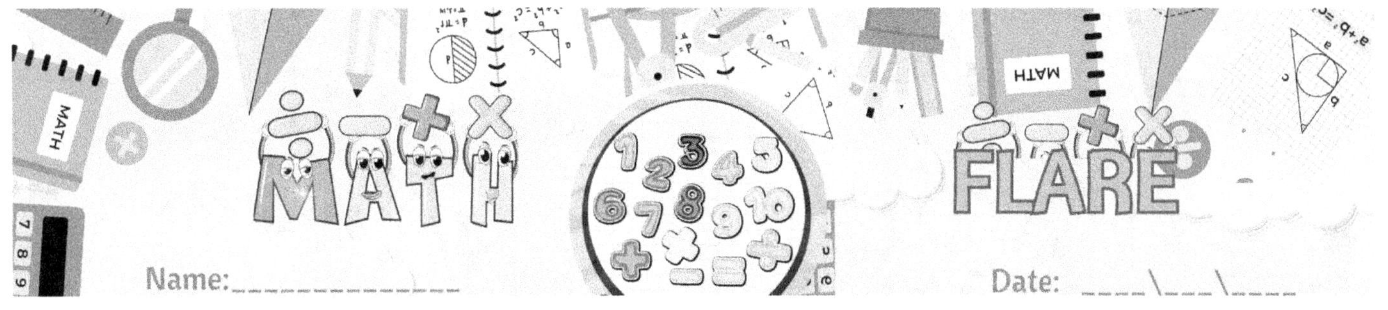

9. $-7x + 4 = 4$

10. $5x + -3 = 7$

11. $2x + 6 = 24$

12. $6x + -2 = -38$

13. $-4x + -4 = -12$

14. $-3x + -5 = -20$

15. $-5x + -5 = -20$

16. $9x + 2 = -61$

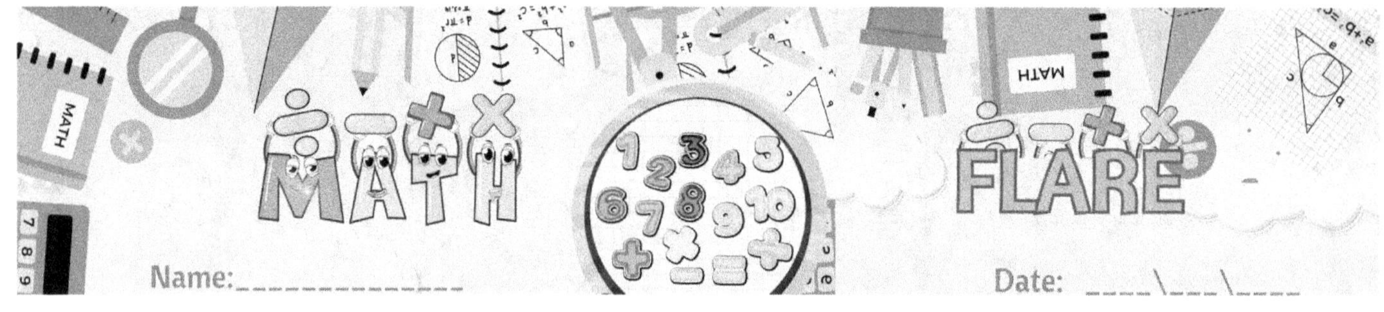

17. -6x + -10 = -16

21. 1x + 1 = -8

18. -1x + 8 = 8

22. 3x + -6 = -33

19. -3x + 0 = 18

23. -3x + 7 = -11

20. -4x + -7 = -35

24. -7x + 5 = -65

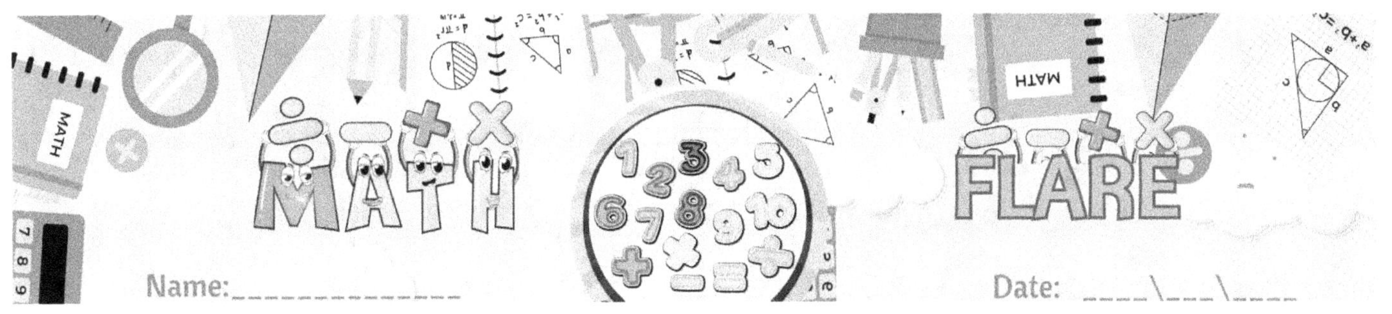

25. $3x + 3 = 24$

26. $-1x + -1 = -4$

27. $10x + -3 = 97$

28. $3x + -5 = 7$

29. $7x + 9 = -19$

30. $3x + 9 = 27$

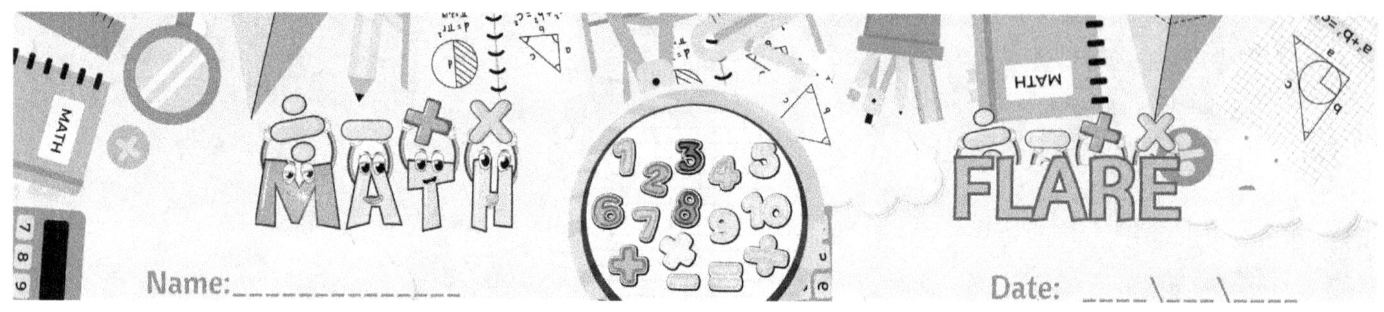

Find Slope from Two Points

1. (5, 58) and (5, 58)

2. (-10, -20) and (2, 16)

3. (9, -81) and (9, -81)

4. (6, 6) and (-7, -7)

5. (3, -27) and (1, -11)

6. (-2, -13) and (3, 12)

7. (9, 73) and (3, 19)

8. (4, -13) and (-5, 14)

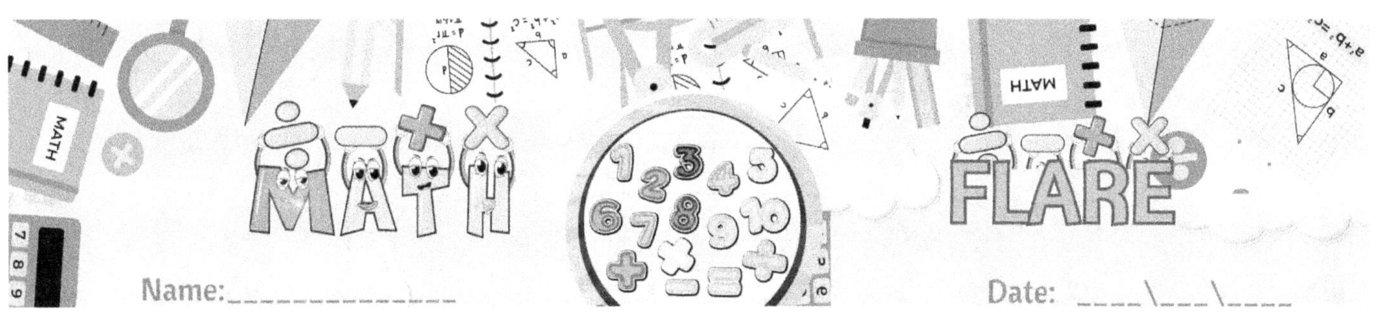

9. (1, -11) and (-3, 21)

13. (-9, -76) and (-7, -58)

10. (3, -18) and (4, -24)

14. (-2, -6) and (9, -28)

11. (7, 34) and (0, -1)

15. (-8, -51) and (-6, -37)

12. (3, 29) and (-10, -88)

16. (7, -45) and (2, -20)

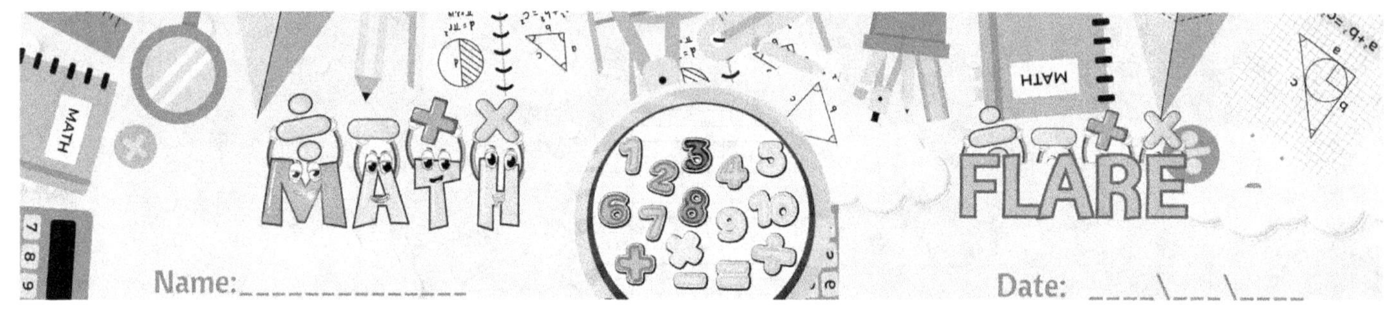

17. (2, 1) and (3, 6)

21. (1, -8) and (-4, 12)

18. (0, 1) and (10, -99)

22. (0, 4) and (7, -10)

19. (-6, 13) and (10, -3)

23. (0, -6) and (6, -48)

20. (-3, -7) and (-5, -15)

24. (-5, 33) and (9, -37)

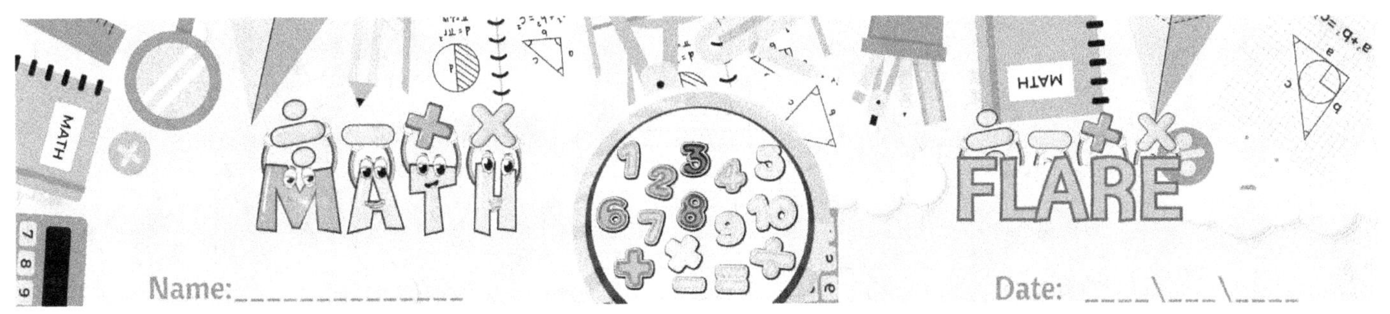

25. (0, -1) and (-2, 13)

26. (0, 1) and (10, -79)

27. (-2, -5) and (-1, -2)

28. (3, -6) and (-9, 30)

29. (3, -32) and (3, -32)

30. (-5, -52) and (-5, -52)

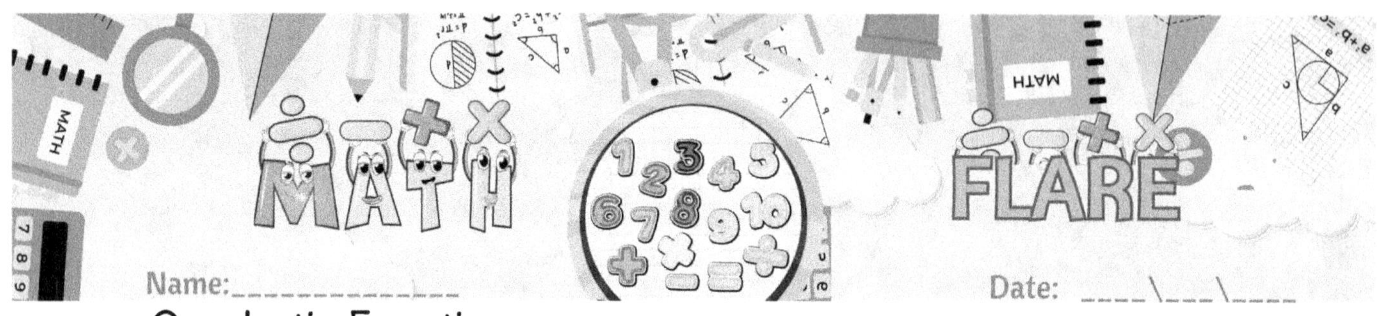

Name:_______________ Date: ____________

Quadratic Equations

1. $5p^2 + 6p - 11 = 0$

2. $-12x^2 + 9x - 1 = 0$

3. $7x^2 - x - 23 = 0$

4. $-4r^2 - 8r + 140 = 0$

5. $-2x^2 - 12x - 4 = 0$

6. $x^2 - 11x - 4 = 0$

7. $b^2 - 25 = 0$

8. $b^2 - 121 = 0$

9. $n^2 - 8n + 16 = 0$

10. $3x^2 - 10x - 112 = 0$

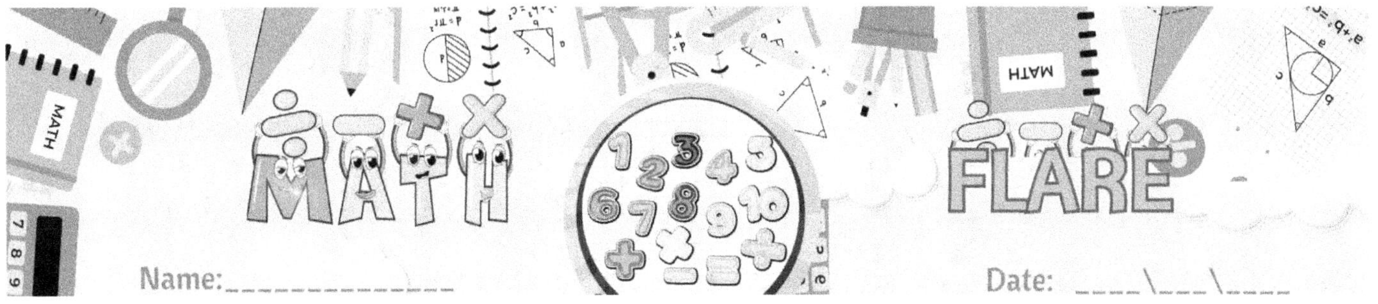

11. $3x^2 + 7x + 4 = 0$

16. $10r^2 + 3r - 9 = 8$

12. $-4r^2 + 5r + 4 = 0$

17. $6m^2 + 3m - 40 = 5$

13. $3x^2 - 9x + 3 = 0$

18. $6x^2 - 2 = 4$

14. $-5n^2 - 8n + 1 = 0$

19. $5v^2 - 9 = 11$

15. $6p^2 - 24 = 0$

20. $6r^2 - 6r - 118 = 2$

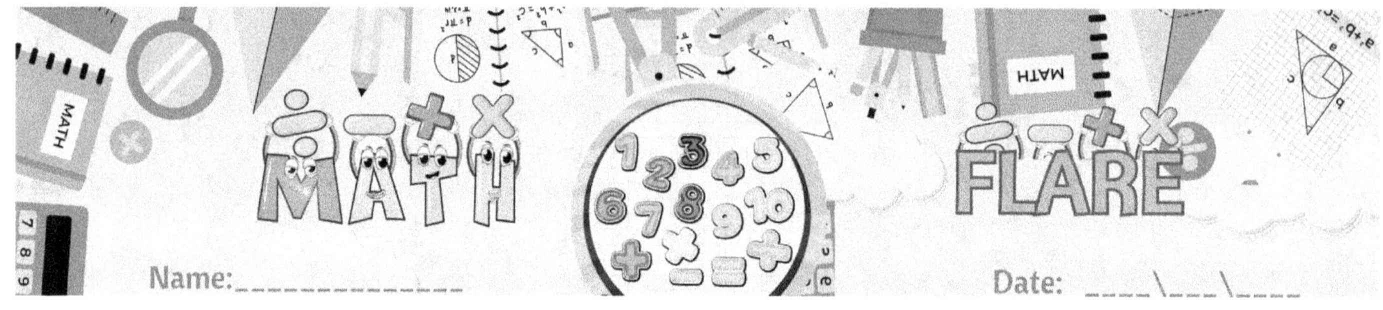

Name:_______________   Date: ____________

21. $6n^2 - 7n - 28 = 10$

26. $6x^2 + x - 110 = 7$

22. $6b^2 + 5b - 110 = -11$

27. $10b^2 - 20 = 4$

23. $n^2 + 8n + 18 = 9$

28. $-8n^2 + 6n + 11 = -4$

24. $4x^2 + 10x + 7 = 3$

29. $-2r^2 + 135 = 7$

25. $-4n^2 - 7n + 4 = 6$

30. $9r^2 - 19 = 3$

31. $-4m^2 - 12 = -m$

36. $12m^2 + 12m = 12$

32. $-6n^2 - 9n = -10$

37. $4k^2 - 12k = 7$

33. $-n^2 + 5n = -66$

38. $12r^2 + 6r = 3$

34. $-9p^2 = -4p + 3$

39. $5x^2 - 4x = 21$

35. $-5v^2 = 7 + 10v$

40. $-6p^2 - 11 = 11p$

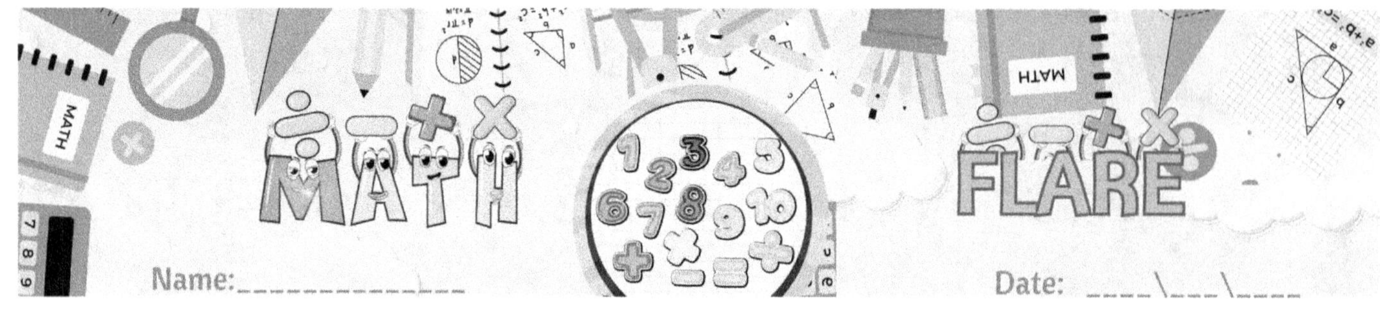

41. $12x^2 - 18 = 4x$

46. $8n^2 + 12n = 17$

42. $-10x^2 - 6 = 10x$

47. $4r^2 - 2 = 7r$

43. $-5b^2 - 9 = 0$

48. $-3v^2 = -7v - 98$

44. $6b^2 = -5 + 12b$

49. $4x^2 - 16 = 0$

45. $-3n^2 = -120 - 9n$

50. $5m^2 = 45$

Name:_______________ Date: ____________

Polynomials: Addition and Subtraction

1. $(5x^4 - x^2) + (6x^4 - 8x^2)$

2. $(3 - 5b) + (4 + 4b)$

3. $(8r^3 - 7r) + (3r^3 - 8r)$

4. $(7r - 2) + (4r - 2)$

5. $(m^4 - 3m) + (8m + m^4)$

6. $(7 + 7v) + (1 - 8v)$

7. $(7p^4 - p^3) + (3p^4 - 6p^3)$

8. $(3x^4 + x^2) - (8x^2 - 4x^4)$

9. $(6x - x^4) + (3x - 7x^4)$

10. $(4r - 5r^3) - (6r^3 + 4r^4)$

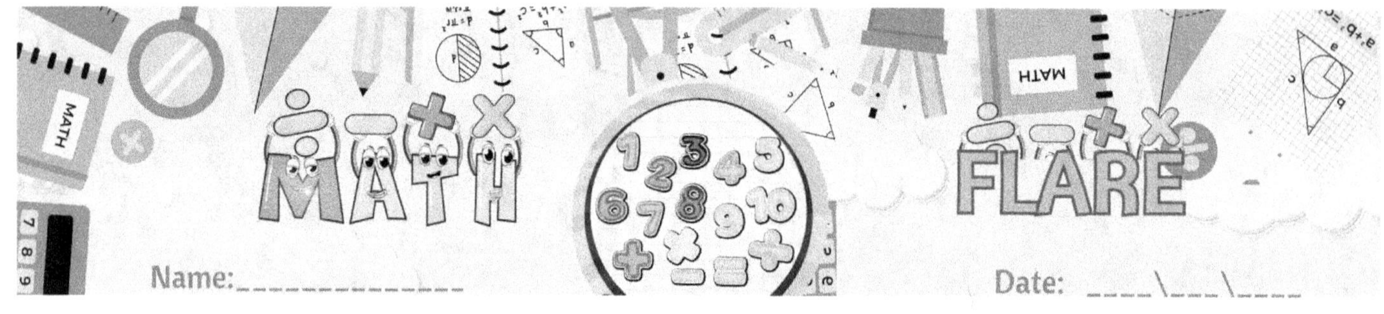

11. $(x + 6x^3) - (2x^2 - 7x^3 + 5x)$

16. $(3x^2 - 3x^4) + (x^4 + 6x + 7x^2)$

12. $(1 + 7k) + (6k^2 + k - 3)$

17. $(8 p^3 + 6 p) + (7 p^4 - 4 p^3 + 7 p)$

13. $(4 p^3 - 4) + (4 p^3 + 6 p + 8)$

18. $(3a^4 - 3a^3) + (6a^4 + 7a^3 - 8a^2)$

14. $(3v - 7v^3) + (7v - 6 - 8v^3)$

19. $(7 + 4v) - (1 + 3v - 7v^3)$

15. $(6v^2 + 8v) + (5 + 5v^2 + 4v)$

20. $(3 p^3 + 4 p) + (3 p + 1 - 4 p^3)$

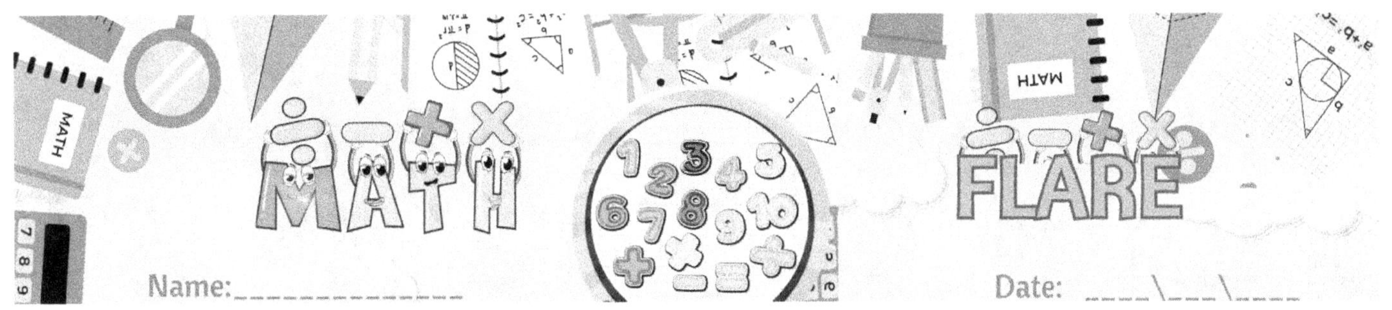

Name:_________________________   Date: _______________

21. $(4x^2 + 8x^4 - 2x) + (8x^2 + 4x^4 - 5x)$

22. $(3p^2 + 8p^3 - 6p) - (5 - 5p^2 - 8p)$

23. $(4x - 1 - 2x^3) - (7x^3 + 4 + 8x)$

24. $(5b^3 + 4b^2 - 2b^4) + (8b^2 - 5b^3 + 7b^4)$

25. $(4b^4 + 6b^2 + 1) + (7b^3 - 6 - 7b^2)$

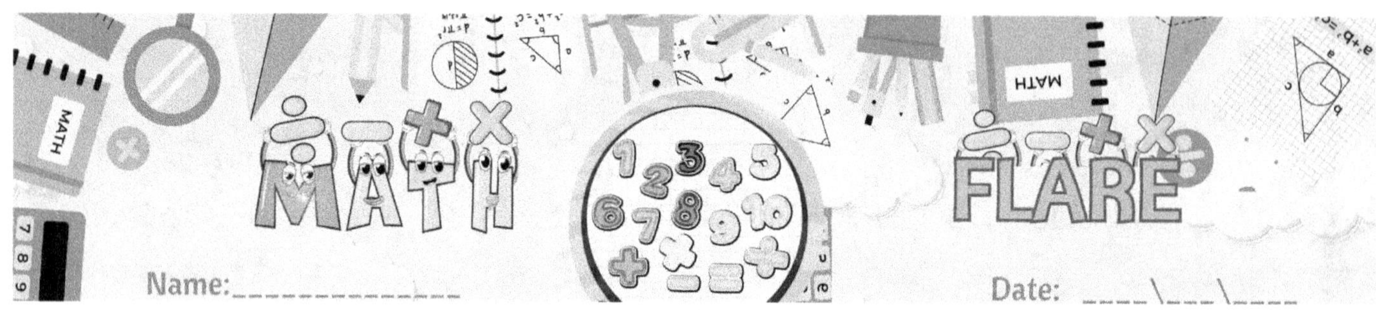

26. $(n - 6n^3 + 7) + (8n + 4n^3 + 7)$

27. $(2 - 3x^3 - x^2) - (5x^3 - 6x^2 - 7)$

28. $(8x^4 - 7x^3 - 6x) - (7x + 2x^3 + 6x^4)$

29. $(5x^4 - 8x^2 + 2x^3) - (5x^4 + x^2 + 5x^3)$

30. $(4n^3 + 7n^2 - 2n) - (6n^4 - 2n + 6n^3)$

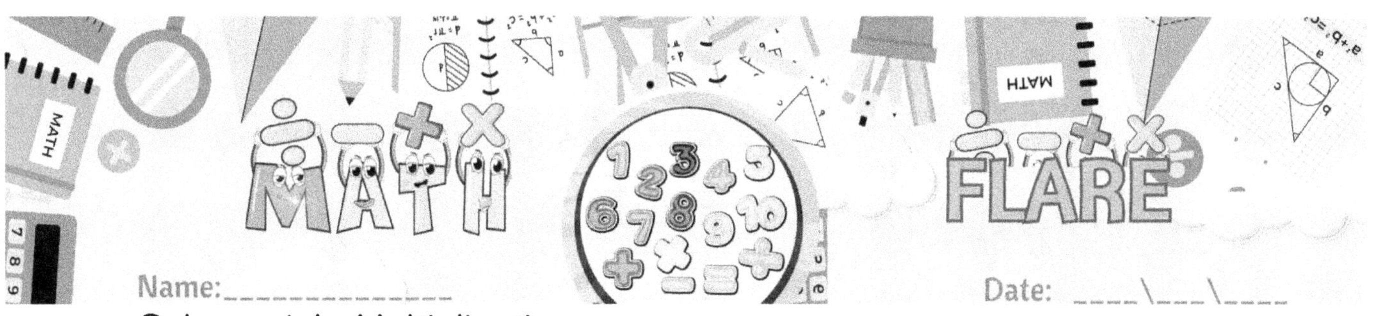

Name:_________________   Date: _______________

Polynomials: Multiplication

1. $(x + 2y)(x + 3y)$

2. $(2x + y)(5x - y)$

3. $(3u + 5v)(4u - 7v)$

4. $(4x + 8y)(3x - 2y)$

5. $(6x - 3y)(8x - 5y)$

6. $(7x - 5y)(2x + 2y)$

7. $(4m - 8n)(8m - 4n)$

8. $(6x + 2y)(3x + 2y)$

9. $(6x + 2y)(8x - 5y)$

10. $(3a + 8b)(2a - 6b)$

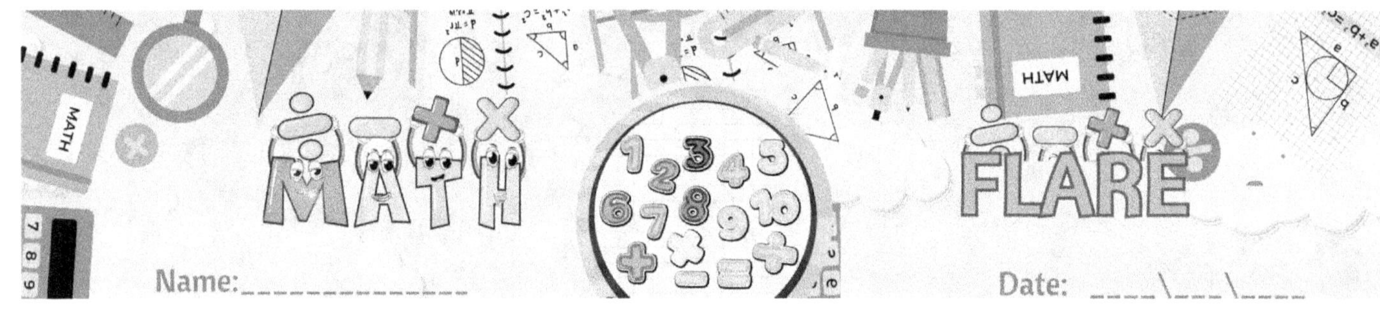

11. $(7x - 6y)(x^2 + 8xy - 5y^2)$

16. $(5u - v)(8u^2 - 2uv - 8v^2)$

12. $(8x + y)(6x^2 + 3xy + 3y^2)$

17. $(7u - v)(2u^2 + uv + 3v^2)$

13. $(3x + 5y)(4x^2 - 3xy + y^2)$

18. $(5x - 7y)(3x^2 + 2xy + y^2)$

14. $(5x + 8y)(x^2 - 6xy - 3y^2)$

19. $(2x - 2y)(7x^2 - 8xy + 2y^2)$

15. $(8x - 4y)(7x^2 - 2xy - 8y^2)$

20. $(7u - 2v)(4u^2 - 3uv + 7v^2)$

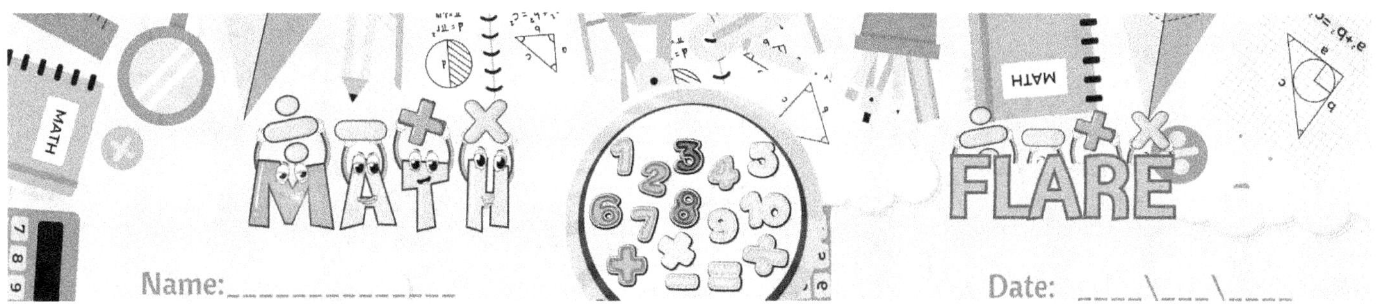

Name:_________________   Date: _______________

21. $(5m^2 + 6mn - 5n^2)(6m^2 + 7mn - 2n^2)$

22. $(x^2 - 7xy + 5y^2)(8x^2 - 2xy + 2y^2)$

23. $(7x^2 - 3xy - 3y^2)(6x^2 - 5xy + y^2)$

24. $(2x^2 + 4xy - 8y^2)(7x^2 - 7xy + 8y^2)$

25. $(6x^2 - xy + 3y^2)(7x^2 - xy - y^2)$

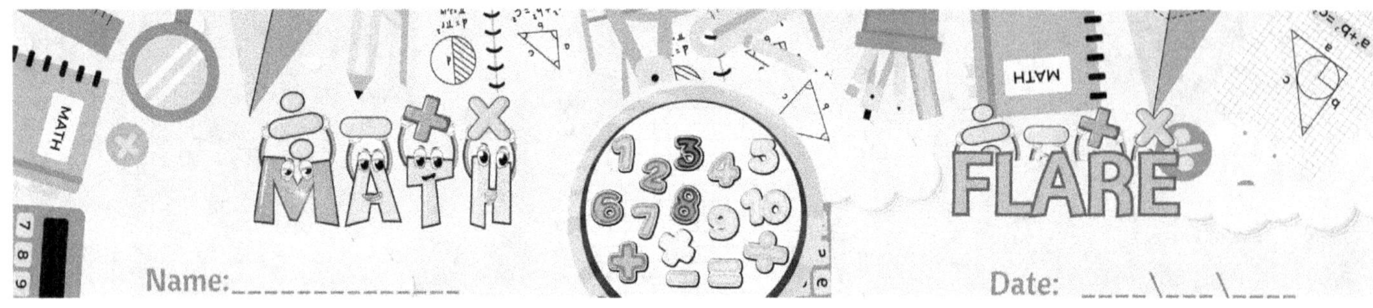

Name:_______________   Date: ______________

26. $(8x^2 + 5xy + 5y^2)(6x^2 - 4xy - 7y^2)$

27. $(3m^2 + 8mn + 8n^2)(6m^2 + 8mn - 3n^2)$

28. $(3m^2 - 2mn + 5n^2)(4m^2 + 4mn + 6n^2)$

29. $(3m^2 + 8mn + n^2)(6m^2 - 3mn - 8n^2)$

30. $(2x^2 + 8xy - 3y^2)(4x^2 + xy - 6y^2)$

ANSWERS

Page 1:   Equations (One Side)

1. k = 4	2. m = 7	3. x = 10	4. k = 6	5. z = 2
6. z = 8	7. y = 1	8. x = 7	9. z = 6	10. y = 7
11. m = 8	12. x = 3	13. x = 10	14. x = 3	15. z = 10
16. y = 3	17. m = 3	18. k = 9	19. z = 5	20. m = 2
21. m = 10	22. y = 5	23. m = 1	24. y = 10	25. k = 4
26. m = 1	27. m = 8	28. z = 7	29. m = 6	30. x = 9
31. m = 4	32. k = 9	33. z = 2	34. k = 4	35. z = 9
36. y = 8	37. z = 4	38. z = 2	39. x = 6	40. x = 9
41. z = 2	42. x = 3	43. m = 7	44. m = 4	45. m = 1
46. z = 8	47. k = 7	48. x = 6	49. k = 5	50. k = 24
51. y = 7	52. m = 4	53. y = 2	54. x = 6	55. k = 8
56. x = 5	57. z = 2	58. z = 5	59. k = 5	60. x = 2
61. y = 8	62. y = 5	63. k = 6	64. x = 8	65. m = 10
66. m = 1	67. y = 2	68. m = 9	69. x = 6	70. k = 3
71. z = 1	72. m = 4	73. y = 4	74. x = 5	75. m = 8
76. y = 5	77. m = 20	78. k = 10	79. m = 10	80. m = 9

Page 8:   Equations (Two Sides)

81. y = 5	82. y = 8	83. z = 7	84. z = 2	85. x = 1	86. z = 2
87. y = 3	88. y = 5	89. z = 3	90. y = 6	91. z = 9	92. k = 9

93. k = 2   94. k = 2   95. x = 7   96. z = 3   97. m = 7   98. y = 7

99. x = 6   100. y = 4   101. z = 6   102. x = 7   103. k = 1   104. z = 8

105. z = 8   106. z = 9   107. x = 3   108. x = 1   109. k = 9   110. k = 8

111. x = 1   112. m = 1   113. k = 7   114. z = 4   115. z = 9   116. y = 2

117. m = 4   118. z = 3   119. k = 6   120. x = 4   121. x = 3   122. z = 1

123. z = 8   124. k = 6   125. k = 1   126. k = 7   127. z = 6   128. x = 2

129. k = 3   130. x = 9   131. k = 4   132. z = 1   133. m = 9   134. k = 9

135. x = 5   136. k = 5   137. y = 8   138. k = 2   139. k = 7   140. y = 1

141. m = 2   142. m = 3   143. x = 5   144. y = 2   145. k = 3   146. x = 5

147. z = 5   148. m = 7   149. k = 4   150. y = 9   151. x = 8   152. x = 8

153. y = 4   154. z = 6   155. k = 6   156. z = 4   157. y = 6   158. z = 8

159. y = 5   160. z = 4   161. z = 5   162. z = 4   163. m = 3   164. x = 7

165. z = 3   166. y = 5   167. k = 6   168. k = 1   169. x = 4   170. y = 5

171. z = 2   172. m = 9   173. z = 1   174. x = 1   175. m = 2   176. m = 2

177. m = 2   178. k = 8

Page 18:   Evaluating Equations

179. 42   180. 15   181. 6   182. 23   183. 5   184. 0   185. 3   186. 42

187. 18   188. 14

Page 19:   Evaluating Equations

189. 2   190. 12   191. 24   192. 1   193. -6   194. -2   195. 15   196. 48

197. 18   198. 23

Page 20:   Evaluating Equations

199. 4   200. 29   201. 12   202. 2   203. 27   204. -2   205. 23

206. 17   207. 55   208. 1

Page 21:   Evaluating Equations

209. 5   210. 24   211. 11   212. 13   213. 11   214. 9   215. 36   216. 4

217. 16   218. 6

Page 22:   Evaluating Equations

219. 9   220. 6   221. -1   222. 9   223. 24   224. 18   225. 9

226. 10   227. 90   228. 2

Page 23:   Evaluating Equations

229. 4   230. 10   231. 6   232. 3   233. -6   234. 28   235. 22

236. -20   237. 12   238. 0

Page 24:   Evaluating Equations

239. 21   240. 5   241. 31   242. -4   243. 130   244. 14   245. 11

246. 20   247. 12   248. 38

Page 25:   Solving Inequalities

249. $x < 13$ 250. $z < 3$ 251. $m > -5/2$ 252. $y \le -6$

253. $x > -3$ 254. $k \le 3$ 255. $z \ge 18$ 256. $y > -1/2$

257. $x < -8$ 258. $z \le 40$ 259. $k < 16$ 260. $m \ge -5/4$

261. $z < -1/3$ 262. $x > 12$ 263. $k \ge 12$ 264. $y > -4$

265. $k \ge -4$ 266. $z \le 4$ 267. $k > -3$ 268. $z \ge 4/3$

269. $y \ge -5/3$ 270. $y \ge -18$ 271. $k \ge 2$ 272. $x < -10$

273. y > -9   274. k ≤ 63   275. y > -4   276. k > -1

277. m ≥ 5/3   278. x ≤ -45   279. m ≥ 2   280. x ≤ 9

281. y ≤ -6   282. x ≥ 5/6   283. k < -35   284. m ≤ -6

285. y ≥ -5   286. k > 3   287. k ≥ 1   288. k < 2

Page 35: Verbal Algebra

289. 9, 72   290. 2   291. 45   292. 5   293. 5   294. 5

295. 0   296. 4   297. 10   298. 12   299. 7   300. 7, 8

301. 14   302. 3   303. 21   304. 6   305. 6, 36   306. 3

307. 16   308. 12   309. 2   310. 0   311. 8   312. 6

313. 10   314. 7   315. 11   316. 50   317. 1, 5   318. 20

319. 8   320. 16   321. 3   322. 10   323. 7   324. 6

325. 1   326. 4   327. 8   328. 9

Page 42: Standard Linear Equations

1. -5	11. 9	21. -9
2. -1	12. -6	22. -9
3. 10	13. 2	23. 6
4. -7	14. 5	24. 10
5. -6	15. 3	25. 7
6. 10	16. -7	26. 3
7. -10	17. 1	27. 10
8. -5	18. 0	28. 4
9. 0	19. -6	29. -4
10. 2	20. 7	30. 6

Page 46: Find Slope from Two Points

1. 10	11. 5	21. -4
2. 3	12. 9	22. -2
3. -8	13. 9	23. -7
4. 1	14. -2	24. -5
5. -8	15. 7	25. -7
6. 5	16. -5	26. -8
7. 9	17. 5	27. 3
8. -3	18. -10	28. -3
9. -8	19. -1	29. -8
10. -6	20. 4	30. 10

Page 50: Quadratic Equations

1. (1, -2.2)	18. (1, -1)	35. No real solution
2. (0.136, 0.614)	19. (2, -2)	36. (0.618, -1.618)
3. (1.885, -1.743)	20. (5, -4)	37. (3.5, -0.5)
4. (-7, 5)	21. (3.167, -2)	38. (0.309, -0.809)
5. (-5.646, -0.354)	22. (3.667, -4.5)	39. (2.488, -1.688)
6. (11.352, -0.352)	23. (-1.354, -6.646)	40. No real solution
7. (5, -5)	24. (-0.5, -2)	41. (1.403, -1.069)
8. (11, -11)	25. (-1.39, -0.36)	42. No real solution
9. (4)	26. (4.333, -4.5)	43. No real solution
10. (8, -4.667)	27. (1.549, -1.549)	44. (1.408, 0.592)
11. (-1, -1.333)	28. (-1.045, 1.795)	45. (-5, 8)
12. (-0.554, 1.804)	29. (-8, 8)	46. (0.889, -2.389)
13. (2.618, 0.382)	30. (1.563, -1.563)	47. (2, -0.25)
14. (-1.717, 0.117)	31. No real solution	48. (-4.667, 7)
15. (2, -2)	32. (-2.243, 0.743)	49. (2, -2)
16. (1.162, -1.462)	33. (-6, 11)	50. (3, -3)
17. (2.5, -3)	34. No real solution	

Page 55: Polynomials: Addition and Subtraction

1. $11x^4 - 9x^2$
2. $-b + 7$
3. $11r^3 - 15r$
4. $11r - 4$
5. $2m^4 + 5m$
6. $-v + 8$
7. $10 p^4 - 7 p^3$
8. $7x^4 - 7x^2$
9. $-8x^4 + 9x$
10. $-4r^4 - 11r^3 + 4r$
11. $13x^3 - 2x^2 - 4x$
12. $6k^2 + 8k - 2$
13. $8 p^3 + 6 p + 4$
14. $-15v^3 + 10v - 6$
15. $11v^2 + 12v + 5$
16. $-2x^4 + 10x^2 + 6x$
17. $7 p^4 + 4 p^3 + 13 p$
18. $9a^4 + 4a^3 - 8a^2$
19. $7v^3 + v + 6$
20. $- p^3 + 7 p + 1$
21. $12x^4 + 12x^2 - 7x$
22. $8 p^3 + 8 p^2 + 2 p - 5$
23. $-9x^3 - 4x - 5$
24. $5b^4 + 12b^2$
25. $4b^4 + 7b^3 - b^2 - 5$
26. $-2n^3 + 9n + 14$
27. $-8x^3 + 5x^2 + 9$
28. $2x^4 - 9x^3 - 13x$
29. $-3x^3 - 9x^2$
30. $-6n^4 - 2n^3 + 7n^2$

Page 59: Polynomials: Multiplication

1. $x^2 + 5xy + 6 y^2$
2. $10x^2 + 3xy - y^2$
3. $12u^2 - uv - 35v^2$
4. $12x^2 + 16xy - 16 y^2$
5. $48x^2 - 54xy + 15 y^2$
6. $14x^2 + 4xy - 10 y^2$
7. $32m^2 - 80mn + 32n^2$
8. $18x^2 + 18xy + 4 y^2$
9. $48x^2 - 14xy - 10 y^2$
10. $6a^2 - 2ab - 48b^2$
11. $7x^3 + 50x^2y - 83xy^2 + 30 y^3$
12. $48x^3 + 30x^2y + 27xy^2 + 3 y^3$
13. $12x^3 + 11x^2y - 12xy^2 + 5 y^3$
14. $5x^3 - 22x^2y - 63xy^2 - 24 y^3$
15. $56x^3 - 44x^2y - 56xy^2 + 32 y^3$
16. $40u^3 - 18u^2v - 38uv^2 + 8v^3$
17. $14u^3 + 5u^2v + 20uv^2 - 3v^3$
18. $15x^3 - 11x^2y - 9xy^2 - 7 y^3$
19. $14x^3 - 30x^2y + 20xy^2 - 4 y^3$
20. $28u^3 - 29u^2v + 55uv^2 - 14v^3$
21. $30m^4 + 71m^3n + 2m^2n^2 - 47mn^3 + 10n^4$
22. $8x^4 - 58x^3y + 56x^2y^2 - 24xy^3 + 10 y^4$
23. $42x^4 - 53x^3y + 4x^2y^2 + 12xy^3 - 3 y^4$
24. $14x^4 + 14x^3y - 68x^2y^2 + 88xy^3 - 64 y^4$
25. $42x^4 - 13x^3y + 16x^2y^2 - 2xy^3 - 3 y^4$
26. $48x^4 - 2x^3y - 46x^2y^2 - 55xy^3 - 35 y^4$
27. $18m^4 + 72m^3n + 103m^2n^2 + 40mn^3 - 24n^4$
28. $12m^4 + 4m^3n + 30m^2n^2 + 8mn^3 + 30n^4$
29. $18m^4 + 39m^3n - 42m^2n^2 - 67mn^3 - 8n^4$
30. $8x^4 + 34x^3y - 16x^2y^2 - 51xy^3 + 18 y^4$